All Hell Can't Stop Them

THE BATTLES FOR CHATTANOOGA: MISSIONARY RIDGE AND RINGGOLD, NOVEMBER 24-27, 1863

by David A. Powell

EMERGING CIVIL WAR SERIES

Chris Mackowski, series editor
Cecily Nelson Zander, chief historian

The Emerging Civil War Series

offers compelling, easy-to-read overviews of some of the Civil War's most important battles and stories.

Recipient of the Army Historical Foundation's Lieutenant General Richard G. Trefry Award for contributions to the literature on the history of the U.S. Army

Also part of the Emerging Civil War Series:

Battle Above the Clouds: Lifting the Siege of Chattanooga and the Battle of Lookout Mountain, October 16-November 24, 1863
   by David A. Powell

Bushwhacking on a Grand Scale: The Battle of Chickamauga, September 18-20, 1863
   by William Lee White

Grant's Last Battle: The Story Behind the Personal Memoirs of Ulysses S. Grant
   by Chris Mackowski

The Great Battle Never Fought: The Mine Run Campaign, November 26-December 2, 1863
   by Chris Mackowski

A Want of Vigilance: The Bristoe Station Campaign, October 9-19, 1863
   by Bill Backus and Rob Orrison

For a complete list of titles in the Emerging Civil War Series, visit www.emergingcivilwar.com.

Also by Dave Powell:

The Chickamauga Campaign. A Mad Irregular Battle: From the Crossing of the Tennessee River Through the Second Day, August 22-September 19, 1863 (Savas Beatie, 2014)

The Chickamauga Campaign. Glory or the Grave: The Breakthrough, the Union Collapse, and the Defense of Horseshoe Ridge, September 20, 1863 (Savas Beatie, 2015)

The Chickamauga Campaign. Barren Victory: The Retreat into Chattanooga, The Confederate Pursuit, and the Aftermath of the Battle, September 21 to October 20, 1863 (Savas Beatie, 2016)

Decisions At Chickamauga: The Twenty-Four Critical Decisions that Defined the Battle (University of Tennessee Press, 2018)

Failure in the Saddle: Nathan Bedford Forrest, Joseph Wheeler, and the Confederate Cavalry in the Chickamauga Campaign (Savas Beatie, 2010)

The Maps of Chickamauga. An Atlas of the Chickamauga Campaign, Including the Tullahoma Operations, June 22- September 23, 1863 (Savas Beatie, 2009)

Union Command Failure In the Shenandoah Valley: Major General Franz Sigel and the War in the Valley of Virginia, May 1864 (Savas Beatie, 2019)

All Hell Can't Stop Them

The Battles for Chattanooga: Missionary Ridge and Ringgold, November 24-27, 1863

by David A. Powell

EMERGING CIVIL WAR SERIES

SB
Savas Beatie
California

Second edition, first printing

ISBN-13 (paperback): 978-1-61121-413-0
ISBN-13 (ebook): 978-1-61121-414-7

Library of Congress Cataloging-in-Publication Data

Names: Powell, David A. (David Alan), 1961- author.
Title: All Hell Can't Stop Them : The Battles for Chattanooga-Missionary Ridge and Ringgold, November 24-27, 1863 / By David A. Powell.
Other titles: All hell cannot stop them
Description: First edition. | El Dorado Hills, California : Savas Beatie LLC, [2018] | Series: Emerging Civil War Series
Identifiers: LCCN 2018040911 | ISBN 9781611214130 (pbk : alk. paper) | ISBN 9781611214147 (ebk)
Subjects: LCSH: Chattanooga, Battle of, Chattanooga, Tenn., 1863. | Missionary Ridge, Battle of, Tenn., 1863.
Classification: LCC E475.97 .P68 2018 | DDC 973.7/359--dc23
LC record available at https://lccn.loc.gov/2018040911

SB

Published by
Savas Beatie LLC
989 Governor Drive, Suite 102
El Dorado Hills, California 95762
Phone: 916-941-6896
Email: sales@savasbeatie.com
Web: www.savasbeatie.com

Savas Beatie titles are available at special discounts for bulk purchases in the United States by corporations, institutions, and other organizations. For more details, please contact Special Sales, 989 Governor Drive, Suite 102, El Dorado Hills, CA 95762, or you may e-mail us at sales@savasbeatie.com, or visit our website at www.savasbeatie.com for additional information.

To historian Jim Ogden and all the staff
at the Chickamauga-Chattanooga National Military Park,
who have been unfailingly supportive of all my work.
It has been a great pleasure to work with them.

Table of Contents

Footnotes for this volume are available at
http://emergingcivilwar.com/publications/the-emerging-civil-war-series/footnotes

This image is a detail taken from the much larger Missionary Ridge Cyclorama that once toured the nation. That Cyclorama was destroyed, but the Wisconsin Historical Society has photographs of the original work. (whs)

List of Maps

Maps by Hal Jespersen

Acknowledgments

In 2017, my first volume for the Emerging Civil War appeared. *Battle Above the Clouds: Lifting the Siege of Chattanooga and the Battle for Lookout Mountain* recounted only half of the struggle that is usually known as the battle (or battles) for Chattanooga. This volume completes that story, examining the Union assault on Missionary Ridge and the Confederate stand at Ringgold, Georgia. For nearly two decades now I have been studying the Civil War in Chattanooga and have received great help along the way.

First and foremost, the man I turn to when I have questions that need answering is Chickamauga-Chattanooga National Military Park Historian James H. Ogden, III. Jim is indefatigable in his efforts to bring attention to the battles for Chattanooga and a well of information on those battles—a well that never seems to run dry. Fittingly, I have thanked him in every book I've written to date; that is as it should be.

A view of the Illinois monument at Orchard Knob as well as cannon that mark Bridges's Illinois Battery. (kw)

I have made many other friends along the way. Park Interpretive Ranger William Lee White has also been of great help and become a good friend. A fellow author for the Emerging Civil War series, he is also author of the foreword for *Battle Above the Clouds*. A trio of William S. Rosecrans and Army of the Cumberland enthusiasts, fellow historians Frank Varney, David Moore, and Joseph Rose have all provided help in setting the record straight on what happened at Chattanooga.

I also wish to thank one other invaluable contributor: Harvey Scarborough, photographer extraordinaire, who—just as he has in the past—supplied many of the modern pictures in this volume. Living as he does in the area and possessed of a fine photographic eye, he has saved my bacon with timely pictures more than once. I am indebted to him for his work and for his ever-cheerful rapid turn-around of my oft-unreasonable demands.

I am indebted to my other colleagues at Emerging Civil War, most especially to Chris Mackowski and Kris White, without whom there would be no Emerging Civil War on the web or in print; and who enthusiastically supported my suggestion to do a book—two books in fact—on the battles

Lookout Mountain as seen from the south end of Missionary Ridge. (dp)

for Chattanooga. They have worked hard to make this project a success. I hope it meets all their expectations.

In my work, I have visited legions of archives, state and local, ranging from universities to local libraries. Too many historical societies and archives languish, underfunded, struggling to meet the demands of historians like myself with limited time and resources. Please seek out and support these institutions wherever you live, for they are essential in producing this book and other books like them.

I wish to also thank the kind folks at Savas Beatie, for making this book possible, and not just as publisher of the Emerging Civil War Series. Theodore P. Savas first took a chance on me as a new author in 2009, with *Maps of Chickamauga*, and subsequently gave me the latitude to fully explore the Chickamauga campaign in detail. Ted, along with Sarah Keeney and the rest of the Savas Beatie staff apply their invaluable skills and talents to make each book a success. I am delighted to be working with them.

Finally, I wish to thank two people who, though neither contributed directly to this book, have been instrumental in their own way. Dr. William Glenn Robertson has always graciously shared information and ideas on Chickamauga and Chattanooga. I have learned much from him. Similarly, I felt myself honored to get to know author and historian Wiley Sword. I started reading Wiley's work while I was still in high school, and it was a great honor to get to know and discuss history with him at meetings of the Historians of the Western Theater. Wiley passed on in 2015, but his work lives on.

PHOTO CREDITS: Abraham Lincoln Presidential Library, Springfield, IL (alpl); *Battles and Leaders of the Civil War* (b&l); Benefiel, *Souviner of the Seventeenth Indiana Regiment* (17th in); *History of the Twentieth Tennessee,* W. J. McMurray, 1904 (20th tn); Library of Congress (loc); *Michigan at Chickamauga and Chattanooga* (mcc); Miller, *Photographic History of the Civil War* (phcw); *Pennsylvania at Chickamauga and Chattanooga* (pcc); Dave Powell (dp); Harvey Scarborough (hs); E. J. Sherlock, *Marches and Battles in which the One Hundredth Regiment of Indiana Infantry Volunteers Took an Active Part. War of the Rebellion, 1861-5, 1896* (ejs); Paul Stanfield, Jr. (ps); Trimble, *History of the Ninety-Third Regiment Illinois Infantry* (hntri); U.S. Army Heritage and Education Center, MOLLUS collection, Carlisle, PA (usahc); Kris White (kw); Wisconsin Historical Society (whs)

For the Emerging Civil War Series

Theodore P. Savas, *publisher*
Chris Mackowski, *series editor*
Cecily Nelson Zander, *chief historian*
Sarah Keeney, *editorial consultant*
Kristopher D. White, *co-founding editor*

Maps by Hal Jespersen
Design and layout by Chris Mackowski

"The grandest stroke yet struck for our country.
Our loss is small considering the exploit.
The Storming of a steep hill five hundred feet
high on a front of two miles, everywhere doubly
entrenched, by a line of troops which soon
lost their formation and streamed upward,
aggregating into channels as a sheet of water
would have done. . . . It is unexampled."

— *Montgomery C. Meigs*

$\mathcal{P}$rologue

Maj. Gen. Halleck,
The fight today progressed favorably. . . . Troops
from Lookout Valley carried the point of the
Mountain and now hold the Eastern slope and
point high up. I cannot yet tell you the amount
of casualties but our loss is not heavy. [Major
General Joseph] Hooker reports 2000 prisoners
taken. . . .

With those words, dispatched to the War Department at 6:00 p.m. on November 24, 1863, Maj. Gen. Ulysses S. Grant acknowledged the Union victory at Lookout Mountain. Though Grant would later downplay that success, dismissing the engagement as a mere skirmish puffed up to feed Joseph Hooker's need for newspaper headlines, on the evening of the battle his satisfaction was evident. General Braxton Bragg's Confederate forces had been dealt a sharp blow.

To be fair, Hooker's assault was essentially an afterthought, hastily converted from a diversion into a full-scale attack only at the last minute on November 23, after a washed-out pontoon bridge at Brown's Ferry stranded Brig. Gen. Peter J. Osterhaus's Federal infantry division from Maj.

A modern view of Chattanooga from the crest of Lookout Mountain. (cm)

Gen. William T. Sherman's column on the wrong side of the flood-swollen Tennessee River. Rather than leave an entire division out of the coming battle, Grant acquiesced to Hooker's plan—a full-fledged attack on Lookout Mountain instead of a mere demonstration—and substituted other troops to join Sherman's intended effort. But still, Grant had little expectation that Hooker would secure any significant result.

As it turned out, the "Battle Above the Clouds" drew every eye, Union and Confederate, on November 24. Though in reality most of the battle was fought within the fog and cloud bank shrouding Lookout's slopes, periodic glimpses of the action could still be seen, as if some great theater curtain was periodically pulled aside to reveal the combat. Henry Yates Thompson, an English civilian who witnessed the affair, left a vivid description of the moment when the United States flag could be seen ascendant:

> We saw Hooker's men fall back once—then they advanced again. After some little suspense we saw the Rebels run around the face of Lookout. . . . An officer beside me with a telescope cried out: There they are and the Rebels are running[!] . . . General Grant watched it all from Fort Wood with General [David] Hunter and Quartermaster-General [Montgomery C.] Meigs. Grant wearing his plain wideawake such as I was wearing and with nothing military about him except a large opera glass. Furious cheering soon started on the Federal right. . . . Above the sound of the popping of the rifles and the roar of the artillery arose a great shout through the whole valley of Chattanooga. From Fort Wood we could see plainly . . . the Union soldiers near the top of the mountain carrying a great Stars and Stripes flag. Now all down the valley right along to the extreme left, where Sherman's men could hardly have known what it was all about, rose the cheers of victory.

Union troops stand atop Lookout Mountain after its capture. In the months following the battle, many a Federal traveled to the summit to have his image photographed or otherwise recorded in warlike splendor. (loc)

The spectators in . . . Chattanooga took up the cry; and I never in my life saw anything like the excitement on Fort Wood. . . . When Hooker's men planted that large U.S. flag . . . the whole of the troops . . . who must number some 60,000 at least, seemed to hurrah together.

For Grant, those cheers were premature. His plans for the battle of Chattanooga were just beginning to unfold, and his most powerful blows had yet to land.

Grant Plans a Battle

CHAPTER ONE
NOVEMBER 18 – 23, 1863

Major General Ulysses S. Grant had other reasons to downplay the importance of Lookout Mountain since he did not expect or plan this fight. As noted, Hooker's affair was meant to be a diversion, fixing Bragg's attention on the Confederate left. The real Union attack on November 24 was supposed to cross the Tennessee River above Chattanooga and seize the north end of Missionary Ridge, assailing Bragg's right. Major General William T. Sherman, Grant's protégé and trusted comrade, led that effort. By the evening of November 24, Grant believed Sherman had fulfilled his mission to the letter. In that same 6:00 p.m. dispatch describing Hooker's success, Grant also reported that "Sherman carried the end of Missionary Ridge and his right is now at the Tunnel and left at Chicamauga [sic] Creek."

Grant was wrong. Sherman had not reached Missionary Ridge on November 24 or even come to grips with Bragg's right flank. This significant mission failure, compounded by Sherman's vague progress reports, left Grant mostly in the dark about the true state of affairs.

To fully grasp the significance of what did—and what didn't—happen on November

The Illinois Monument at Orchard Knob marks the area where the Union generals gathered to watch most of the battle of Chattanooga. (hs)

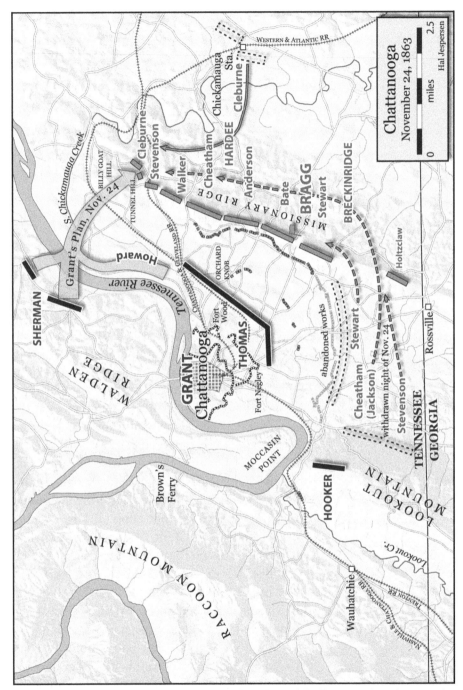

CHATTANOOGA—Grant intended to use Sherman and the Army of the Tennessee to make a surprise crossing of the Tennessee River upstream from Chattanooga, then move quickly to seize the north end of Missionary Ridge and threaten the rail connections there. In doing so, he would isolate Confederate General James Longstreet's forces in East Tennessee. The other two main components of Grant's army, however, under Generals Thomas and Hooker, would have very little to do.

Having relieved the siege of Chattanooga, Maj. Gen. Ulysses S. Grant (left) was still concerned with Burnside, in Knoxville, and intended to strike his next blow sooner rather than later. To strike that blow, Grant turned to his most trusted subordinate, the excitable, irascible Maj. Gen. William T. Sherman, now in command of the Army of the Tennessee (right). (loc)(loc)

24, it is important to look at Grant's original intentions. Grant arrived in Chattanooga with two missions: break the Rebel stranglehold on the besieged Union Army of the Cumberland and ensure Union Maj. Gen. Ambrose Burnside could continue to hold East Tennessee. Burnside, who occupied Knoxville back in September, had mostly cleared East Tennessee of Confederate forces by October—a project near to President Abraham Lincoln's heart. East Tennessee opposed secession; thousands of East Tennesseans donned Union blue to help put down the rebellion. Here, Lincoln's loyal Southerners eagerly waited to see secession undone; Lincoln felt East Tennessee could be the model for reconciliation going forward. Once Bragg isolated Chattanooga, however, Burnside's position appeared tenuous.

Things grew more desperate for Burnside and his men in early November when, at Confederate President Jefferson Davis's orders, Bragg detached Lt. Gen. James Longstreet and 20,000 troops toward Knoxville. Longstreet intended to capture or drive out Burnside once and for all. Though hindsight reveals Longstreet's force never possessed sufficient strength nor supplies needed to accomplish that mission, President Lincoln worried about this development. In fact, prompted by Lincoln in early November, Grant ordered Maj. Gen. George H. Thomas to peremptorily attack Bragg, hoping to either force Longstreet's recall or defeat Bragg outright.

Thomas protested his army was unprepared to launch any kind of attack, and Grant ultimately called off the effort. Burnside would have to fare for himself a while longer.

On November 18, Grant issued his orders. As described, the main blow would be delivered against Bragg's right at the north end of Missionary Ridge. Sherman, leading 25,000 men from Grant's trusted Army of the Tennessee, would deliver the blow. This strategic thinking soundly analyzed the situation and possible outcomes. If Sherman seized the north end of Missionary Ridge, Grant would have also inserted a wedge between Bragg's army and Longstreet's expeditionary force, allowing Grant to defeat each portion of the Rebel army in detail. To further ensure Longstreet's isolation, Grant authorized a Union cavalry raid against Cleveland, Tennessee; this raid would destroy the East Tennessee Railroad track and depot there, and if possible, take out the rail bridge over the Hiwassee River. Such destruction would prevent both information and reinforcements from flowing between Bragg and Longstreet, gaining enough time for Grant's men to win the battle at Chattanooga.

However, this plan left most of the 85,000 Union troops gathered at Chattanooga out of the fight. As noted, Hooker's attack on Lookout Mountain was originally intended to be a diversion, not a full-scale assault. In fact, driving the Confederates off Lookout Mountain might be counterproductive, since its capture would collapse the Rebel defensive line across Chattanooga Valley and force Bragg to considerably shorten his existing lines. Oddly, Bragg clung to Lookout Mountain through the month of November, a mysterious action since after the night action at Wauhatchie and the re-opening of the Cracker Line, the Rebels derived no military advantage from the position. Prestige and morale reasons left Bragg loath to give up the

With the loss of Lookout Mountain and Chattanooga Valley, Gen. Braxton Bragg could no longer lay any claim to successfully besieging Chattanooga, and there was very little strategic sense in his remaining outside Chattanooga. Retreat, however, was not a viable political option, leaving the Army of Tennessee precariously perched on Missionary Ridge. (loc)

mountain, but he surely grasped that his few troops could not adequately defend this extended line.

Grant, the new Federal commander, also grasped the overextended nature of Bragg's line and chose not to worry about reclaiming Lookout Mountain. Instead, he ordered Maj. Gen. Joseph Hooker to merely demonstrate in front of the mountain, pantomiming an assault to divert Bragg's attention away from Sherman. Hooker's diversionary role prompted Grant to reduce that officer's command to fewer than 10,000 men, insufficient for a full-scale assault. Only after the pontoon bridge at Brown's Ferry washed out on November 23,

leaving Brig. Gen. Peter J. Osterhaus's division of the XV Corps stranded on the wrong side of the river and unable to re-join Sherman in a timely fashion, did Grant relent and allow Hooker to make more of his demonstration if circumstances allowed. For Hooker, this was all the authorization he needed. The resulting "Battle Above the Clouds" won a spectacular Union triumph, though not one Grant had expected or planned.

Charles A. Dana, pictured here a year later in Virginia, was one of a number of important observers gathered in Chattanooga to watch the battle. Dana served as assistant secretary of war to Edwin M. Stanton, providing Stanton with a confidential pipeline into Grant's headquarters. (loc)

What about the single largest contingent of Grant's command, George Thomas's Army of the Cumberland? "You will cooperate with Sherman," wrote Grant, further instructing Thomas to mass most of his available force "on your left flank . . . [with] a moveable column of one division in readiness to move whenever ordered. This division should show itself as threateningly as possible on the most practicable line for making an attack. . . ." Thomas's mission called for bluffing and only joining the attack when Sherman secured Missionary Ridge "to about the railroad tunnel."

Thus, from his 85,000 available troops, Grant intended to attack with only 25,000 men, relegating the remaining 60,000 to a diversionary role, distracting Bragg while Sherman did the main work. This plan hardly seemed in keeping with Lincoln's admonishment to the Army of the Potomac's leadership after the Fredericksburg debacle: "Gentlemen, in your next battle, put in all your men."

Why? Simply put, Grant distrusted the Army of the Cumberland. He believed that after Chickamauga their fragile morale would not stand aggressive action. He attributed—unfairly, as it turned out—Thomas's real reason for inaction earlier in the month to this fragility, not to the stated logistical shortcomings. Grant hesitated to stake the coming battle on their perceived lack of resolve. As he told Sherman on November 15, Grant fretted "that the men of Thomas's army had been so demoralized by the battle of Chickamauga that he feared they could not be got out of their trenches to assume the offensive."

One additional factor complicated Grant's planning: concern that Bragg might suddenly retreat, abandoning the Confederate's over-stretched forward line for a more defensible position near Ringgold. James Longstreet indeed had proposed this sound idea prior to his departure for Knoxville. If Bragg pulled off this move now, it would disrupt Grant's plans, allowing the Rebels to escape unscathed. On the morning of the twenty-third, Assistant Secretary of War Charles A. Dana, observing affairs in Chattanooga, passed on Grant's concerns in a 10:00 a.m. dispatch to the War Department:

Quartermaster General Montgomery C. Meigs was also present in Chattanooga, helping to organize Grant's supplies. His contemporaneous private journal provides a useful window into the Union high command at the time. (loc)

Evidence that Bragg is retreating from Chattanooga to a line covering the communications of Longstreet accumulates. . . . A lieutenant of the Thirty-Seventh Tennessee Infantry, who deserted Saturday [November 21] reports that everything in Bragg's lines indicated retreat. Yesterday [Sunday] the railroad east of Missionary Ridge was unusually active . . . [and] troops and trains were seen moving eastward over the ridge. . . . Last night two deserters came in at midnight reporting that Bragg's artillery had all been sent off; that the trains were all ordered in from up Chattanooga Valley; that the troops were moving off, and that by this evening only a picket line would be left here in our front.

Thus, the heavy lifting fell to Sherman, who, by all indications, needed to act quickly. That same Monday, November 23, despite the bridge washout that stranded Osterhaus's men, Grant set things in motion. Sherman's remaining three divisions, reinforced by Maj. Gen. Oliver O. Howard's XI Corps and one division of the XIV Corps, began final preparations for their own assault, crossing the Tennessee River above Chattanooga, opposite the mouth of South Chickamauga Creek. In the meantime, Grant ordered Thomas to drive in the aforementioned Rebel picket line centered on Orchard Knob, a mission easily accomplished that afternoon. Set for dawn on November 24, Sherman's crossing and Hooker's diversion would begin the new conflict.

Sherman Stumbles

CHAPTER TWO
NOVEMBER 24, 1863

Sherman began his task well enough. On the night of the twenty-third, Sherman's three Army of the Tennessee divisions (Brig. Gen. Morgan L. Smith's 2nd and Brig. Gen. Hugh Ewing's 4th divisions of the XV Corps, accompanied by Brig. Gen. John E. Smith's 2nd Division of the XVII Corps, about 13,000 men in all) camped in the hills on the north side of the Tennessee River, behind Stringer's Ridge, concealed from enemy observation. The 6,200 men of Brig. Gen. Jefferson C. Davis's 2nd Division, XIV Corps, held the river bank at Sherman's intended crossing point, assembling the pontoon boats needed for the assault; artillery batteries positioned themselves on the bank to lend support when needed. Howard's small XI Corps, 6,400 strong, waited within the Union lines on the south bank, preparing to move north and establish overland contact once Sherman's column crossed.

Just before midnight, the 55th Illinois and 8th Missouri infantry from Morgan Smith's command began boarding 116 pontoon boats, 25 men to a boat. They embarked in North Chickamauga Creek, floating out into the Tennessee and then downstream to land on the south bank, just above

A modern view of Billy Goat Hill from the southeast. Confederate skirmishers opposed the Federal advance from this valley. (hs)

Hugh Ewing was both William Sherman's foster brother and brother-in-law. Sherman considered him his most reliable division commander. (loc)

Patrick Cleburne was one of the Army of Tennessee's most able divisional commanders. Irish-born, with prior enlisted service in the English Army, Cleburne later emigrated to Arkansas. He would prove his worth repeatedly over the next few days. (b&l)

the mouth of South Chickamauga Creek. They achieved near-perfect surprise, capturing all but one of the Rebel pickets and with only a single shot fired, "that by the last sentinel," recorded the 55th's regimental historian, "but this caused no alarm to the enemy."

Immediately, the Federals entrenched, having brought the necessary tools. The boats began ferrying the rest of Morgan Smith's division across while pontoniers started assembling a bridge. By dawn, both Morgan Smith's and John Smith's formations, some 8,000 men, had disembarked, and the rest expected to be over the river soon.

Hugh Ewing's large, three-brigade division came next. Ewing (who also happened to be Sherman's brother-in-law and former law partner) led his division forward after dawn, the crossing now aided by the steamboat *Dunbar*. Formerly a Southern craft sunk dockside in Chattanooga by Union artillery fire back in August, the raised and repaired *Dunbar* now plied her trade for the men in blue. Ewing's troops went into position on the right flank, allowing John E. Smith to both push the bridgehead forward another 500 yards and pull one of his brigades back into reserve, readying for the next phase of the attack.

Jefferson C. Davis's command arrived last, along with most of the artillery. By now, the congestion was considerable. Brigadier General John Beatty, heading one of Davis's brigades, noted that by the time he reached the bridge, "there were many troops in advance of us, and my brigade did not reach the south side [of the Tennessee] until after one o'clock." Once across (and following Grant's warning about the Army of the Cumberland's lack of offensive ardor), Sherman ordered Davis's troops into reserve. To connect Sherman's men with George Thomas's Army of the Cumberland, Col. Adolphus Bushbeck's brigade of the XI Corps also marched up the river road past the Crutchfield plantation,

along the south bank of the Tennessee, eventually joining their picket lines with Ewing's.

Bragg largely ignored this crossing. Even though his right was virtually unprotected, his attention seemed wholly fixed on his left, where Hooker stormed Lookout Mountain. The existing Confederate line on Missionary Ridge ended south of the Chattanooga & Cleveland Railroad tunnel, well short of the northern end of the ridge. Bragg had been forced to shorten his lines, sending Buckner and Cleburne to reinforce Longstreet. On November 23, after the Federals seized Orchard Knob, Bragg reversed himself enough to recall all Cleburne's men and one brigade of Buckner's. Now, Cleburne's division stood in reserve on the east side of Missionary Ridge, behind Bragg's headquarters at the Moore house.

Early on the morning of the twenty-fourth, Bragg and members of his staff rode north from his headquarters to inspect those portions of his lines on Missionary Ridge now held by Brig. Gen. States Rights Gist's division; there, through the intermittent drizzle, Bragg caught his first

This view of Tunnel Hill and Missionary Ridge, taken from the west in the 1890s, shows the railroad leading to Missionary Ridge Tunnel. This is the view Federal troops would have had when assaulting the ridge later in the morning of November 25. (pcc)

Marcus J. Wright's brigade of Tennessee infantry was dispatched to oppose Sherman's crossing. Wright was not a popular or very successful commander; in 1864, he would be assigned rear-area duties. His greatest contribution to the war would be between 1878 and 1917, when he was employed by the War Department to gather and organize Confederate documents for the publication of the *Official Records*. (20th tn)

sight of Sherman's force. His initial response to Sherman's appearance, however, merely ordered Cleburne "to send a brigade and a battery to the East Tennessee and Georgia Railroad Bridge over the Chickamauga to guard that point."

At 8:30 a.m., Bragg also ordered Brig. Gen. Marcus J. Wright's brigade—newly detrained at Chickamauga Station from East Tennessee, the last of Cheatham's men returning—to leave one regiment to guard the railroad bridge over the Chickamauga at Shallowford, and with the other three regiments, "proceed toward the mouth of the Chickamauga to develop the strengths and designs of the enemy. Resist him every step. Should he not have crossed the Tennessee, resist his crossing."

The sum of Bragg's response? Just two brigades, and only one of those did he send directly to resist Sherman: Three regiments sent Bragg to oppose 25,000 men. Understandably, Wright chose to proceed with great caution. At noon, Bragg, apparently satisfied, rode toward Lookout, leaving Lt. Gen. William J. Hardee in charge of the Rebel right.

Fortunately for Braxton Bragg, Sherman took his time. Though his orders were to attack and capture the north end of Missionary Ridge, and though he met with no opposition, Sherman spent the entire morning entrenching while the last of his forces completed the crossing. Grant, at Orchard Knob, observed this sluggish action with the appearance of calm detachment. His only sign of impatience came at 11:20 a.m. In that dispatch, Grant informed Sherman that "considerable movement has taken place on top of the ridge toward you . . . [but] until I do hear from you I am loath to give any orders for a general engagement. Hooker seems to have been engaged for some time, but how I have not heard. Does there seem to be a force prepared to receive you . . . ? Send me word what can be done to aid you."

At 1:30 p.m., Sherman finally ordered an advance, each division abreast, in column of brigades. Morgan Smith moved on the Union left, alongside and south of Chickamauga Creek; John Smith held the center while Ewing, echeloned slightly to the rear, held the right. Bushbeck's XI Corps men screened Ewing's flank while Davis remained in reserve. Their intended objective waited two miles away.

This full-scale movement finally woke Bragg and Hardee to the peril. At 2:00 p.m., Patrick Cleburne, still holding his remaining three brigades in reserve behind the ridge, received two breathless couriers at virtually the same moment. Hardee's man relayed an order directing Cleburne to the vicinity of the railroad tunnel, where "an officer of General Hardee's staff . . . would show me my position." Bragg's man "told me I must preserve the railroad bridge in my rear . . . at all hazards." Galvanized, Cleburne left his column to follow, rode quickly to meet Hardee, and observed the lay of the land.

At 3:00 p.m., Sherman's leading elements scaled the highest point ahead of them, climbing onto what they thought was the northern end of Missionary Ridge. Once there, however, Brig. Gen. Joseph Lightburn made a startling discovery: "upon arriving at the summit I perceived it not to be the hill specified in the order." Instead, Lightburn captured a separate piece of high ground, known locally as "Billy Goat (or sometimes just Goat) Hill." Ahead of them the ground fell away again across another valley before rising to Tunnel Hill, where the Confederates now reformed.

These Texan Rebels, commanded by yet another Smith, Confederate Brig. Gen. James A. Smith of Cleburne's command, hurried to their new positions. Though Cleburne managed to get a line of infantry atop that height in the nick of time, his troops were still badly over-stretched.

James A. Smith was a West Pointer, class of 1853, and a native Tennessean, though he commanded a brigade of Texans. He was promoted to brigadier general a week after the battle of Chickamauga. (phcw)

Giles A. Smith was the younger brother of his divisional commander, Morgan L. Smith, and an effective, competent officer in his own right. Badly wounded on November 24, he returned to command in 1864, where he won laurels at the battle of Atlanta for his stubborn defense of a critical position. (loc)

William J. Hardee, nicknamed "Old Reliable," was Bragg's most competent corps commander, though Bragg and Hardee rarely got along. In 1855, Hardee authored the *Manual for Rifle and Light Infantry Tactics*, which became the most common instructional manual for troops on both sides. (loc)

Likely if the Federals had pressed forward in strength, Tunnel Hill would have fallen. Instead, Sherman's advance ground to a halt. As he and his men scrambled into position, Texas Capt. Samuel T. Foster noted that "while we are trying to get located in among these hills and mountains, the Yanks fire upon us before we get in position; but done no damage. The fireing [sic] kept up until dark. . . ."

At 3:30 p.m., when Sherman reached the crest of Billy Goat Hill, he examined the situation, equally nonplussed. His maps, indicating the ground was all one continuous ridge, not separate heights, were clearly wrong. Sherman apparently made little effort to secure local guides, who might have steered him better. Instead of pressing forward, Sherman decided that "the ground we had gained, however, was so important that I could leave nothing to chance, and ordered it to be fortified during the night."

Why did Sherman elect to stop and dig in? Admittedly, daylight waned, but few of his troops had even pulled a trigger. Aside from the encounter with Cleburne's Texans, Sherman's men had only met resistance from Wright's small Tennessee brigade, which had been slowly moving west along the north bank of Chickamauga Creek when Sherman ordered the advance. These Confederates had bumped into Brig. Gen. Giles Smith's brigade, also of Morgan Smith's division, in a collision which caught both sides by surprise. One Tennessean scornfully recollected that they "were marched right along into close contact with the enemy without heed to repeated warnings which were given to our commander." After a limited engagement, Wright fell back to a hill overlooking the north bank of the creek. Wounded, Giles Smith turned brigade command over to Col. Nathan Tupper. The incident certainly drew Sherman's attention. He reported that "the enemy felt our left flank about 4 p.m., and a pretty smart engagement with muskets and artillery ensued, when he drew off." Did Sherman fear his own flank was exposed?

Whatever the reason, Sherman's astounding decision and order to halt ran contrary to Grant's intentions. Despite Sherman's assessment, Billy Goat Hill was essentially meaningless since other heights to the south and east secured the Rebel flank. Seizing it did nothing to turn Bragg's right or threaten the rail station behind Missionary Ridge, but Sherman ordered it fortified. All idea of attack seemed forgotten. Grant's intended main effort had come to nothing.

Or almost nothing. Often overlooked in the story of Sherman's activities on November 24, his advance allowed a Union mounted force of roughly 1,000 troopers, commanded by Col. Eli Long of the 4th Ohio Cavalry, to slip across the river and head for Cleveland, Tennessee. They aimed to cut telegraph wire and tear up as much railroad track as possible, hoping to prevent a timely recall of any more of Longstreet's force. Long's mission concluded successfully, seizing Cleveland on the twenty-fifth, pushing up toward the Hiawassee River the next day, and returning safely to Union lines on the twenty-seventh— after the issue at Chattanooga had been settled.

Fatal Indecision

CHAPTER THREE

NOVEMBER 22-24, 1863

The Bragg Reservation, featuring the Illinois Monument. Before the creation of Interstate 24, Crest Road ran straight here, through what is now the parking lot. (dp)

For two months, Braxton Bragg had wrestled with planning his next step. After the battlefield victory at Chickamauga on September 20, 1863, the city of Chattanooga initially seemed ripe for taking, if the Confederates would only reach out and grasp it. But the Federals proved resilient, rebounding quickly and digging in, turning their works at Chattanooga into a daunting earthen fortress. Reluctant to test those defenses with the lives of his men, Bragg looked for alternate strategies but found limited options.

Bragg's dilemma lay in the fact that while any frontal assault on the Union defenses encircling the city was likely to be a bloody failure, the Confederates lacked the strategic mobility to conduct an offensive turning movement deep into the Union rear, into Middle Tennessee. Yes, Bragg's numbers had swollen to 70,000 men (from roughly 40,000 in August), but he lacked the wagons to keep them supplied more than a few miles from his railhead. As a result, Bragg remained passive, only sending cavalry to strike at the Federal supply line and hoping terrain and worsening weather would starve out the Yankees.

That hope dashed at the end of October

Braxton Bragg, looking younger and far less careworn in this image than in the one on page 4, taken after Missionary Ridge. (loc)

James Longstreet, on loan from the Army of Northern Virginia, soon became one of Bragg's most truculent detractors. When Jefferson Davis suggested that Longstreet be sent to East Tennessee, Bragg jumped at the chance. (b&l)

when the Federals established the "Cracker Line," returning the Army of the Cumberland to full supply. As if to highlight their logistical shortcomings, the Rebels managed only a feeble response, producing the night action at Wauhatchie, a sharp, limited encounter that, from the Confederate perspective, failed to achieve anything useful.

After Wauhatchie, Braxton Bragg again re-evaluated his options and again came up wanting. He had to deploy his army to face multiple threats. Roughly 45,000 troops occupied the encircling heights around Chattanooga, principally the line of Missionary Ridge and the looming crag of Lookout Mountain. Another 15,000 men had been sent to Charleston, in East Tennessee; they were to make sure that another Union army under Maj. Gen. Ambrose Burnside did not approach from Knoxville to attack Bragg's own force from the rear. Bragg's cavalry, about 10,000 troopers under Maj. Gen. Joseph Wheeler, ranged even more widely, from north Alabama to eastern Tennessee. Wheeler's men and animals, worn out from their recent raid and reduced by crippled horses, had limited effectiveness; the command's real numbers remained uncertain, even to army headquarters.

Bragg's attempt to starve out the Yankees failed. A direct assault remained out of the question. In early November, seeking another way to lever the Federals out of Chattanooga, Bragg agreed to a plan conceived by Confederate President Jefferson Davis: send Lt. Gen. James Longstreet and 20,000 troops against Burnside at Knoxville.

For Bragg, the scheme also appealed since it rid him of a man he considered a key troublemaker. Longstreet had been at the center of a near-mutiny in the ranks of the Confederate generals serving under Bragg. The mutineers included Leonidas Polk and Thomas C. Hindman, whom

Bragg had placed under arrest for disobedience at Chickamauga, Daniel Harvey Hill, whom Bragg relieved of command in late October, and Simon B. Buckner, whom Bragg demoted from corps to divisional command. The generals' conflict escalated badly, forcing President Davis to travel west, spend several days with the army in October, and resolve the crisis personally. Davis partially sustained Bragg, arranging a transfer instead of a court-martial for Polk, getting the charges against Hindman dropped, and bringing in William J. Hardee to replace Hill. Of the key conspirators, only Longstreet remained unscathed, but relations between Bragg and him were virtually non-existent.

Simon Bolivar Buckner, a sometimes-corps commander in the Army of Tennessee and another Bragg opponent, was suddenly tasked with reinforcing Longstreet outside of Knoxville on November 23. This proved to be one of Bragg's worst decisions of the campaign. (loc)

Unfortunately for Confederate hopes in East Tennessee, Bragg and Longstreet continued to see things differently. Longstreet expected to join his troops with the force already in East Tennessee, giving him 30,000 to 35,000 men and a significant numerical advantage over the Federals. Bragg, mindful of the growing Yankee numbers in Chattanooga, intended Longstreet to replace the East Tennessee force, which would be recalled to the main front. Even worse for Longstreet's expectations, he discovered Bragg could offer him no additional logistical support, leaving Longstreet to improvise a supply train from locally confiscated, meager transportation. Unsurprisingly, these efforts culminated without crowning success. Later, many of Longstreet's troops looked back on their time in East Tennessee as the greatest hardship they endured during the war, a time when they lacked everything necessary to keep an army in the field.

Most of November passed, with Longstreet slogging his way toward Knoxville and Bragg watching the steadily increasing Federal numbers at Chattanooga. The troops recently returned from East Tennessee, two divisions commanded by Maj. Carter L. Stevenson, were first assigned

Ambrose Burnside commanded the Union forces at Knoxville. Though his reputation was damaged by his poor handling of the battle of Fredericksburg, he proved to be a capable and effective commander in East Tennessee. (loc)

to the defense of Missionary Ridge at Tunnel Hill, but on November 12, re-assigned to defend Lookout Mountain. Stretched for numbers, Bragg chose not to send replacements to Tunnel Hill.

Unexpectedly, on November 22, Bragg changed course. Impatient with the slow results at Knoxville, Bragg decided to reinforce Longstreet with two more divisions, "nearly 11,000" men, commanded by Maj. Gen. Patrick Cleburne and Brig. Gen. Bushrod R. Johnson—in temporary charge of Simon Buckner's command. Bragg also knew Sherman's troops had reached Chattanooga but appeared to be readying to march north, up the Tennessee River. The Confederate commander interpreted this movement as an effort to either attack Longstreet from the rear or place a Federal wedge between the two Rebel commands. Either way, Bragg decided to act. Overnight, both Cleburne and Johnson moved to Chickamauga Station where trains waited to carry them to Loudoun, Tennessee. Johnson's men led the movement.

As described previously, General Grant interpreted this movement as a general retreat, touching off the Union advance against Orchard Knob late that morning. From his headquarters atop Missionary Ridge, Bragg could see the full panoply of this movement, with rank after rank of Federal infantry venturing forth. The Confederate general realized he could not weaken the Army of Tennessee by sending troops to Longstreet.

Cleburne, supervising the movement toward Longstreet, reported that he "had sent off all of Buckner's Division except [Brig. Gen. A. W.] Reynolds's brigade when I received the following order . . . 'you will halt such portions of your command as have not yet left . . . ; such as may have left halt at Charleston.'" As directed, Cleburne immediately ordered Reynolds's Tennessee brigade to detrain and sent word to Bushrod Johnson to stop his movement at Charleston. Two more directives arrived in rapid succession: the first ordered "Johnson's troops at Charleston back here." The second, hard on the heels of the first, informed Cleburne that "we are heavily engaged. Move up rapidly to these headquarters."

As it turned out, Bragg's army was not "heavily engaged," except for the handful of Alabamians defending Orchard Knob; the Union attack stopped once they had driven in Bragg's picket line. As a result, Bragg changed his mind again. Bushrod Johnson, who was at Charleston struggling to get everyone started back toward Missionary Ridge, "received a dispatch . . . to the effect that the order for the return of troops . . . only applied to such of my troops as had not left Chickamauga [Station] and that I would proceed as previously ordered."

Instead of 11,000 more men, two full divisions, Longstreet would get barely 2,500, two small brigades. Of necessity, now Bragg turned some attention to his own defenses. He did not, however, turn that attention to either re-occupying Tunnel Hill at the north end of Missionary Ridge or to withdrawing his over-extended line from Lookout Mountain. Instead, he decided again to await Grant's next moves.

Those moves came the very next day. Sherman crossed the Tennessee at dawn to move against Bragg's undefended right while Hooker assailed Lookout Mountain. For Bragg, the main effort seemed to be against his left, at Lookout, where the Yankees captured the Cravens House Plateau and pushed around the mountain far enough to threaten Summertown Road. If they blocked that road, then Carter Stevenson's remaining two brigades at the mountain's summit would be trapped, forced to march miles south to rejoin the main army. Now, Bragg had no choice except to abandon Lookout, ordering Stevenson's

Maj. Gen. George Thomas, one of whose nicknames was "Old Slow Trot," was a methodical, careful commander. He and Grant repeatedly differed on strategy concerning how best to attack the Confederates besieging Chattanooga, leaving Grant to doubt the Army of the Cumberland's effectiveness. (loc)

Ulysses S. Grant, as sketched by a member of the 32nd Indiana Infantry, Adolph Metzner. It captures Grant's calm demeanor. (loc)

whole force back to Missionary Ridge. He also abandoned the line of Confederate works stretching across Chattanooga Valley between the mountain and Missionary Ridge—by controlling Lookout's lower slopes, Hooker's infantry column had completely enfiladed those defenses and could take them easily from the flank or rear.

Tunnel Hill and the Rebel right flank remained largely an afterthought for most of the day until Sherman resumed his advance in the afternoon. Even then, Sherman's groping, slow progress allowed Bragg to dispatch troops to deal with the threat, dispatching first a couple of brigades, later the rest of Cleburne's division. When oncoming dusk closed the battle, the Confederates had Tunnel Hill—the key to Bragg's right—well-defended and would strengthen its defenses overnight.

Bragg took one final step to strengthen his position on November 24, ordering a new line of defensive works dug atop the ridge. Before, the Confederate lines had been down in the valley in front of the ridge, to besiege the Union defenders. Now, outnumbered and threatened with attack, Bragg finally thought to erect a fallback position. Those new defenses, hastily constructed at the last minute, proved sadly incomplete when they became a needed part of the Confederate position.

Raid on Cleveland

CHAPTER FOUR

NOVEMBER 24 - 27, 1863

"Brig. Gen. George Crook: Select from your command a brigade of 1,500 to 2,000 men under command of Col. E. Long, and start them so as to reach here by Saturday next at noon. They are wanted for an important raid."

With those words, sent on the night of November 16, Gen. George Thomas lay the groundwork for an often overlooked but key element of the Union plan: keeping Longstreet and Bragg separated once operations began in earnest. The man chosen to lead this mission, Eli Long, had served pre-war as a Regular from the 1st and 4th U.S. cavalries and during the Civil War took command of the 4th Ohio Cavalry after Stones River. Born in Kentucky, Long had not attended West Point, graduating instead from the Frankfort Military Institute, in 1856, and securing a direct commission as a lieutenant. He proved his worth in revitalizing the 4th Ohio and held brigade command through much of 1863.

Long and his men belonged to the Army of the Cumberland's 2nd Cavalry Division, which in early November picketed the Tennessee River in northern Alabama, between Huntsville and Stevenson. On the move since June—first taking part in the Tullahoma Campaign, then

This monument to the 1st Ohio Cavalry commemorates its service at Chickamauga, September 1863. The monument sits near the site of the Widow Glenn house and Wilder Tower at Chickamauga. (rc)

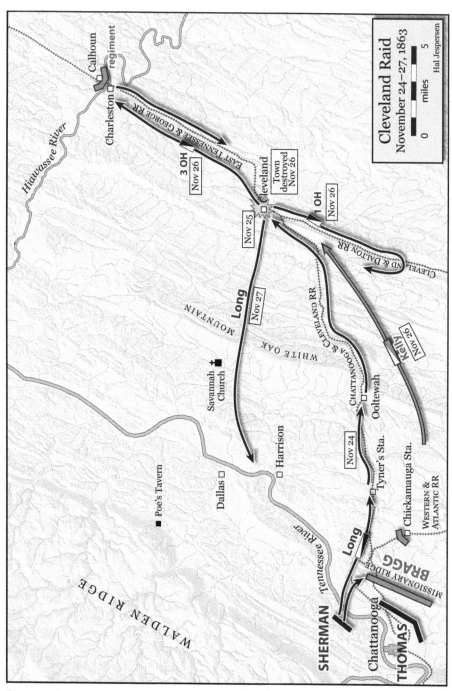

CLEVELAND RAID—The Union cavalry raid on Cleveland, Tennessee, was one of the most important such strikes of the war. Grant's primary objective was to sever the rail line, thus ensuring that James Longstreet would not be able to quickly return from East Tennessee. As an added bonus, Eli Long's troopers destroyed the South's only copper rolling mill, necessary to make percussion caps.

Chickamauga, and most recently pursuing Confederate cavalryman Joe Wheeler through much of east and middle Tennessee—the blue cavalry was worn out. Now, with many mounts in need of rest and unfit for field work, Long's brigade built winter quarters. "This was an innovation for the regiment," recalled William Curry of the 1st Ohio, "as we had never had anything of the kind before, and the boys began to congratulate themselves that they were going to have a quiet winter campaign."

Long departed for Chattanooga on November 18. "Saturday next" was November 21, four days ahead. He divided the regiments; only the most fit men and mounts would go. To make up the required 1,500 men, Long drew in detachments from other brigades. In total, he commanded parts of 1st Ohio, 3rd Ohio, 4th Ohio, and 4th Michigan cavalry regiments, and elements of the 17th Indiana and 98th Illinois Mounted Infantry. The column reached Chattanooga a day late, delayed by the same difficult roads that plagued Sherman, and crossed the Tennessee at Brown's Ferry on November 22. Since Grant had already postponed the offensive, the extra delay mattered little.

Eli Long, a little-known but effective Union cavalry commander, led the Federal raid against Cleveland, Tennessee. According to historian Ezra J. Warner, in his career Long was "awarded every brevet in both the regular and volunteer services ... up to and including the grade of major general." (phcw)

Here, Long received his final instructions. The commands ordered his ad-hoc brigade to cross the Tennessee River on November 24, behind Sherman's column, and then make for Cleveland, "and destroy as far as possible the enemy's lines of communication in that direction." Since four divisions of Union infantry crossed ahead of them, Long's troopers spent most of November 24 as spectators. Sergeant W. H. H. Benefiel of the 17th Indiana recalled they spent most of the day on Stringer's Ridge, "the identical spot" where they and the 18th Indiana Battery first fired on Chattanooga back on August 21, 1863. Now, Benefiel reminisced, "we could plainly see the outlines of Hooker's gallant men as they

W. H. H. Benefiel and his wife, pictured after the war. Benefiel, who suffered from poor health due to his service injuries, was employed by the U.S. Indian service from 1889 to 1893, and again from 1898 to 1909. (17th in)

charged up over [the] craggy slopes till they were hidden from our view by the rain-cloud. . . . Still we could plainly hear the crack of the small arms, as well as the cheering by our noble boys as they would drive the Johnnies from point to point."

Once the bridge cleared, Long's column crossed in turn and struck out for Tyner's Station on the Chattanooga & Cleveland Railroad, which lay just east of Missionary Ridge. There, they paused just long enough to tear down the telegraph wires and capture the civilian operator before pushing on. Long's men marched 13 miles that evening, stopping repeatedly to rip down the telegraph wires and to damage the railroad "by burning and tearing up the track." The column halted to rest at midnight, "with orders not to unsaddle our horses, as we were in the immediate rear of the rebel army."

Long's force did not pass unnoticed. Confederate Brig. Gen. Marcus Wright's brigade of Tennesseans operated in the area, in addition to a small brigade of Rebel cavalry under Kentucky Col. J. Warren Grigsby. Grigsby's mission was to screen the Confederate right flank, since Bragg lacked the force to defend the

ground between Missionary Ridge's northern terminus and the river. Wright, it will be recalled, briefly tangled with Giles Smith's brigade of Federals and then retreated northward. During this action Wright heard from Grigsby, who informed him that "a large force of [the] enemy's cavalry had succeeded in crossing the river . . . in the direction of Tyner's Station." At 9:00 p.m., Wright withdrew back to Chickamauga Station, avoiding any collision with Long's troopers, thanks to "Col. Grigsby's knowledge of the ground." Less fortunate, Wright's brigade trains stumbled directly into Long's encamped column at about 2:00 a.m. They were promptly captured and destroyed, with "severe loss" in both private and army property.

Long had his men moving again before dawn on the twenty-fifth, leaving Wright's captured wagons blazing behind them. His target, Cleveland, lay only 16 miles distant. The Federals wreaked considerable additional destruction along the way. An advance party of the 4th Michigan had already seized the small settlement of Ooltewah, where they captured 17 Rebels, destroyed 4,000 pounds of requisitioned flour, and burned a railroad bridge. The day's

This image shows a Union bridge being built across the Tennessee River at Bridgeport, but bridges like it were put in place at Brown's Ferry and at South Chickamauga Creek for Sherman's use. That bridge carried Long's Cavalry across the Tennessee on November 24. (loc)

biggest capture came later in the morning when they stumbled across another train of 52 Rebel wagons. "After taking all that we could use of the supplies," noted Sgt. Thomas Crofts of Company C, the 3rd Ohio Cavalry, "we burned the train and . . . marched to Cleveland."

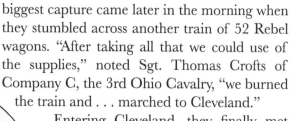

Entering Cleveland, they finally met organized resistance, though of a limited nature. Grigsby sent 250 men of the 2nd Kentucky Cavalry under command of Lt. Col. Thomas G. Woodward to hold the place, but they proved no match for Long's numbers. The 1st Ohio led the way into town, and Woodward's Rebels retreated. According to Ohio Sgt. Alvin Thompson of Company D, they discovered the real prize of the campaign that night "when two soldiers of Co. D found a warehouse full of tobacco, and by daylight, every man in the company had from 20 to 200 plugs to take back to Chattanooga to sell to the infantry." More importantly for the Union war effort, Colonel Long sent out patrols in preparation for movements the next morning.

Confederate cavalry commander John H. Kelly had only recently been transferred from infantry service, having led a brigade of that arm at Chickamauga. Only 23 years old when he received his brigadier general's commission on November 16, 1863, Kelly was the youngest Confederate general officer in the service. (phcw)

November 25 proved to be the decisive day of the actions collectively known as the battle of Chattanooga, the day Bragg's infantry were driven off Missionary Ridge in ignominious retreat. Long's troopers had no idea of that success until they returned to Chattanooga days later, but their presence certainly disrupted Confederate plans. James Longstreet learned most of his expected reinforcements would not be arriving because of Long's endeavors. On the twenty-fifth, in perhaps one of the last dispatches to get through between the two Confederate commanders before Federals yanked down miles of telegraph, Longstreet lamented that "your dispatch informed me that two divisions were ordered [to join me.] I now learn that it is two brigades that may come, and without artillery."

One of Long's patrols proved especially worrisome. Brigadier General Bushrod Johnson waited at Loudon, about 40 miles northeast of Charleston, where the railroad bridged the Hiwassee River. By 5:00 p.m., Johnson passed disturbing news to James Longstreet: "The enemy's cavalry," Johnson wired, "are in sight of Charleston and moving on the bridge. . . . We have but one regiment at Charleston."

With most of Joseph Wheeler's cavalry helping Longstreet besiege Knoxville, the Confederates were poorly positioned to deal with Long. Only Brig. Gen. John H. Kelly's small division of two brigades—including Colonel Grigsby's— protected Bragg's right flank as far as Charleston, but the fighting at Chattanooga required they be in multiple locations at once. Grigsby's men remained to protect Bragg's right flank, including Tyner's and Chickamauga stations. Kelly scraped together a small force of 500 men in three regiments drawn from Col. William B. Wade's brigade, added a battery of artillery, and set off for Charleston to defend the rail bridge.

On November 26, Colonel Long concentrated on inflicting maximum damage. Dividing his force, he ordered detachments down the rail lines south toward Dalton, back east toward Tyner's, and north toward Charleston. Each force concentrated on ripping up track and bending the iron rails by heating them over bonfires of crossties. Scouring Cleveland, Long reported that he destroyed "a considerable lot of rockets and shells, large quantities of corn, several bales of new grain sacks, . . . several railroad cars . . . [and] the large copper rolling mill—the only one of the kind in the Confederacy." The 1st Ohio also "destroyed ten miles of the Dalton track."

The most significant damage was the loss of the copper rolling mill. Built in 1861 by German immigrant Julius E. Raht to service the nearby copper mines at Ducktown in Polk County,

For most of the campaign, Union cavalry was assigned a defensive role, guarding the Tennessee River or various depots. The lack of horseflesh was also a problem. The troopers on the ridge behind the train likely gathered at the railroad depot in Chattanooga well after Eli Long's raid on Cleveland. (loc)

Tennessee, the Confederate government seized the rolling mill and mining operation under the Sequestration Act of 1861, considering it vital to the Southern war effort. Raht, no secessionist, refused to swear loyalty to the new government, lost his ownership, but stayed to manage the business and provide what protection he could for his disenfranchised investors. Copper, an essential war material to produce many things, was especially important for rifles' and pistols' percussion caps.

William Le Roy Broun, head of the Confederate arsenal in Richmond, admitted with the loss of this resource, "the casting of bronze field guns was immediately suspended, and all available copper was carefully hoarded for the manufacture of caps. It soon became apparent that the supply would be exhausted and the armies rendered useless unless other sources of supply could be obtained." Ultimately, the South cannibalized turpentine and brandy stills, sending purchasing agents amid great secrecy to seize or buy those stills wherever they found them. "Thus," Broun admitted, "all the caps issued from the arsenal . . . during the last twelve months of the war manufactured from the copper stills of North Carolina."

While their comrades wreaked havoc in town, Lt. Col. Charles B. Seidel led the 3rd Ohio Cavalry, supported by two companies of mounted infantry, back to Charleston. Their objective targeted the railroad bridge spanning the Hiwassee River at Calhoun. They "found [that] the enemy occupied Calhoun with infantry and artillery," reported the regimental history, "had a skirmish; tore up some railroad track, returning to Cleveland in the afternoon." The bridge remained undamaged.

November 27 brought a more determined Confederate response when Brig. Gen. John H. Kelly led his 500 Rebels into town. Picket firing erupted as early as 2:00 a.m., but Kelly waited to initiate a full attack until after dawn while Long's men breakfasted. Though Long had depleted his strength by detachments, including the sending of the 4th Michigan back to Chattanooga with prisoners, he still retained a sizeable numbers advantage over Kelly. He lacked artillery, however, which Kelly possessed, and Long knew he was behind enemy lines with potentially many more Rebels converging on his position.

Long retreated, an orderly operation by Union accounts, less so by Confederates' accounts. Seventeen-year-old Cleveland resident Myra Inman exulted that "our forces attacked Gen. Long's forces, 13 hundred strong, and whipped them. We had 2 cannon and a howitzer, 2 or 3 killed on both sides, several wounded." More ominously, Kelly's Rebels would not stay because, as they informed her, "Bragg has fallen back."

By the evening of the twenty-seventh, the Yankee cavalry returned to the banks of the Tennessee River north of Chattanooga where they learned what transpired in their absence: The battle of Missionary Ridge.

The Fight for Tunnel Hill

CHAPTER FIVE
NOVEMBER 25, 1863—MORNING

Despite Sherman's unexpected foot-dragging, the Army of Tennessee had a rough day on November 24. After Hooker's success at the Cravens House, Bragg now had no choice except to abandon Lookout Mountain since the crest was indefensible with the lower shelf in Union hands. This also meant a collapse of the Confederate line in Chattanooga Valley, vulnerable to being turned by Hooker's column. The Rebel left fell back to Missionary Ridge, with Bragg's new flank anchored on Rossville.

Patrick Cleburne, whose timely appearance saved Tunnel Hill and prevented the collapse of Bragg's right, expected the army would begin a more general retreat after dark. "Accordingly," he reported, "[I] had sent my ordnance and artillery across" the Chickamauga, except for one section of two guns. Much to Cleburne's surprise, after midnight Capt. Irving Buck of his staff—who had been sent to Bragg to inquire about new orders— brought word that the army would "await the enemy's attack on Missionary Ridge." Cleburne recalled his artillery and set his infantry to work more fully fortifying Tunnel Hill.

Bragg's decision to stay came after an

A modern view, taken from the Confederate position on Tunnel Hill, looking north along the spine of the ridge. The Iowa Monument in the distance marks the position of Corse's brigade. (dp)

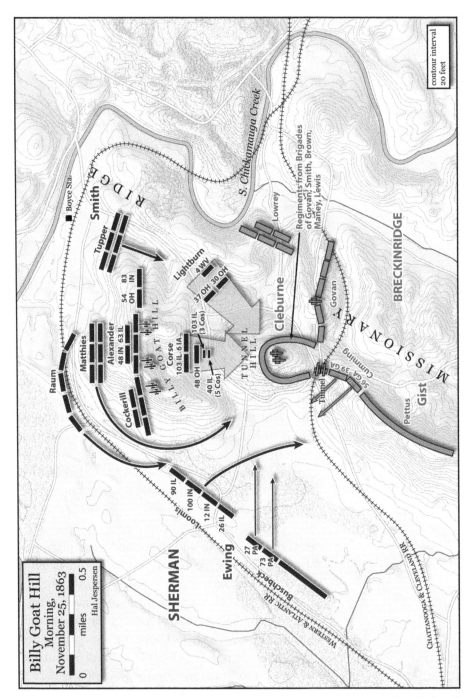

BILLY GOAT HILL—William T. Sherman's attacks against Tunnel Hill on the morning of November 25 lacked coordination and strength. Troops were committed a brigade at a time, and Confederates easily repulsed them.

evening conference with his corps commanders, Lt. Gen. William Hardee and Maj. Gen. John C. Breckinridge. Despite his quasi-independent command on Lookout, Maj. Gen. Carter Stevenson normally commanded a division, subordinate to Breckinridge, and thus was not present. Colonel George Brent of Bragg's staff noted at the time that both corps commanders felt an immediate retreat would be difficult to organize and argued that the army must stay, at least for a time. But Hardee contended they should at least fall back to Chickamauga Station, "about four miles east of the ridge," while Breckinridge, impressed with the natural strength of the ridge, argued, "if the army could not make a stand on such favorable ground as it then held, it could not do so anywhere." Bragg agreed.

John C. Breckinridge was yet another officer on the outs with Bragg. Despite that animosity, Breckinridge rose to corps command after the departure of D. H. Hill, relieved in October. Though he performed well both before and after Missionary Ridge, his rash argument to defend instead of retreat swayed Bragg and led to disaster. (loc)

Brigade commander Arthur Manigault's post-war recollections, combined with Brent's journal, suggest Bragg did intend a retreat, just not that night. He needed more time to organize a rearward move, to shift stockpiled supplies southward, and to get the army trains well to the rear. Manigault even thought the movement commenced and then halted; like Cleburne, he initially did not expect the army to fight it out on Missionary Ridge on November 25. When orders to fortify the top of the ridge arrived, he was greatly surprised.

Overruled on the idea of retreat, Hardee pointed out that if he defended the north end of Missionary Ridge, he must be reinforced. Cleburne's men alone could not hold the length of ground. Bragg agreed, directing Cheatham's and Stevenson's divisions, already pulling back from Lookout Mountain, to move beyond Breckinridge's portion of the line and report to Hardee. With Captain Buck, Hardee sent a final warning to Cleburne: "Tell Cleburne we are to fight; that his division will be heavily attacked, and they must do their very best."

This stark view of Missionary Ridge, taken in 1864, shows the denuded nature of the ridge at the time of the battle. After months of occupation by the two opposing armies, timber was scarce, most of it used for fuel and earthwork construction. (loc)

Grant took similar stock of his fortunes. He also expected Bragg to retreat, and the heavy movements conducted on the Confederate side of the battle lines beginning after dark seemed to suggest that very thing. Accordingly, his orders for November 25 intended to either forestall any withdrawal or at least strike the enemy while in mid-move.

Grant had a flawed grasp of this tactical situation. The fault largely lay with William Sherman, who proved evasive about what, exactly, had been accomplished on November 24. Sherman failed to inform Grant about his lack of progress or about the error concerning Billy Goat Hill. In fact, in his overnight orders, Grant informed George Thomas that "General Sherman carried Missionary Ridge as far as the tunnel, with only slight skirmishing. His right now rests at the tunnel, and on top of the hill, his left on Chickamauga Creek." This information, completely incorrect, gave a false picture of the situation. Sherman was not on Missionary Ridge nor was his right "at the tunnel." Instead, a Confederate infantry division held the northern end of Missionary Ridge with another division on the way.

Based on Sherman's report, however, Grant decided the Union Army of the Tennessee would continue the main effort on the twenty-fifth. "I have instructed General Sherman to advance as soon as it is light . . . and your [Thomas's] attack, which will be simultaneous, will be in cooperation. . . . Your command will either carry the rifle pits and ridge directly in front of them, or move to the left [toward Sherman] as the presence of the enemy may require." These orders directed Thomas and his men to either take Missionary Ridge, if the Rebels had left only a rear guard to hold it while escaping, or, better yet, pin Bragg's army in place while Sherman finished up the job, striking it in the flank.

Hooker's role was equally conditional. On the night of the twenty-fourth, Confederates still held the top of the Lookout Mountain, and Union commanders did not know with certainty their enemy would choose to abandon that position. Accordingly, Hooker's first task focused on securing the Summertown Road, which would isolate any Rebels remaining on the crest; only then he might move eastward to strike the south end of Missionary Ridge at Rossville.

John M. Corse and his brigade were selected to lead the first Union attack against Missionary Ridge. He spent two years at West Point, but did not graduate, and later became an Iowa lawyer. (loc)

Dawn brought dramatically different climate conditions. The previous day's fog, rain, mist, and clouds dissipated. Day broke clear and cold, though a little haze lingered in the valleys. This visibility yielded panoramic views. Shortly after sunrise, the national flag waved atop Lookout Mountain. Six men, led by Capt. John C. Wilson, from the 8th Kentucky Infantry of Walter C. Whitaker's brigade planted that first flag. Before first light, Wilson recalled, "we crept cautiously upward, clutching at rocks and bushes. . . . At every step we expected to be greeted with deadly missiles . . . ." Instead, they discovered the vacant summit. Wilson positioned the colors on the very

Alfred Waud's dramatic sketch of Corse's attack on the morning of November 25 shows Sherman's view of that advance from Billy Goat Hill, looking toward the end of Missionary Ridge. (loc)

tip of Lookout's brow, visible to every Federal in Chattanooga. Other flags followed close behind, including the 29th Pennsylvania's and—to ensure everyone knew who should get the real credit – John Geary's White Star divisional banner. Union morale soared. One blue-clad private, viewing the banner from Orchard Knob, supposedly exulted, "Look at old Hooker. Don't he fight for keeps?"

Grant and Thomas soon realized that while Bragg had abandoned Lookout, the Rebels still held Missionary Ridge. The Union generals observed the Confederates manning two lines: the works at the foot of the ridge and a new line of hastily constructed defenses at the top of the crest.

These morning revelations induced Grant to modify his plans in two important ways: First, with Lookout liberated, he ordered Hooker to leave a minimum force to hold the mountain and press on for Rossville. Second, Thomas no longer needed to launch what would now likely be a bloody frontal assault; the Army of the Cumberland could accomplish Grant's goal and fix the enemy in place merely by threatening to charge. Instead, Sherman's and Hooker's attacks would assail Bragg's flanks. After all, Sherman already—at least according to what Grant knew—waited astride the ridge's northern end. Thomas's men could deliver the *coup de grace*, should one be needed, once both Bragg's flanks turned.

That morning Sherman had four divisions under his immediate command: Morgan Smith's, John Smith's, and Hugh Ewing's, all from the Army of the Tennessee, and Jefferson Davis's, from the Army of the Cumberland. Sherman also controlled Col. Adolphus Buschbeck's brigade of the XI Corps, which had moved up on Sherman's right flank after he crossed the Tennessee to establish a west bank link with the main army in Chattanooga. The rest of the XI Corps stood nearby in support, four more brigades in two divisions, with orders from Thomas to "conform to the movements of General Sherman." Excepting Howard, this force amounted to nearly 24,000 men. Morgan Smith's division occupied Billy Goat Hill. John Smith and then Hugh Ewing extended that line to the right while Buschbeck posted farther south on Ewing's right. Together, they formed a semi-circular line focused on Tunnel Hill, now well defended by Cleburne's Confederates. The Northerner Davis and the bulk of Howard's force, posted farther to the rear, formed on the open plains nearer the Tennessee River. Sherman had plenty of strength to call on, if needed.

Bragg had moved more slowly, and morning found his dispositions far from complete. Carter Stevenson's division had started moving to fill in on Cleburne's left, extending the Rebel formation southward along the crest of Missionary Ridge, but as of dawn, only the first of Stevenson's four brigades had reached position. The remainder were still marching and would be moving throughout the morning. One of Cleburne's brigades, led by Col. Mark P. Lowrey, occupied a second ridgeline just east and a bit north of Tunnel Hill. From there, Lowrey's and Stevenson's men protected Cleburne's right flank and could deliver a crossfire on any of Sherman's men advancing south toward Tunnel Hill. As further flank support, Marcus Wright's Tennessee brigade was stationed behind (east of) Lowrey, defending the rail bridges (for both the Western & Atlantic and Chattanooga & Cleveland lines) over South Chickamauga Creek. Once all of Stevenson's men arrived, the Confederates would number about 13,000 men, considerably fewer than Sherman had at his disposal but well-deployed on advantageous terrain.

By his own report, Sherman acknowledged Grant's original attack order had reached him "about midnight" of November 24. First light of November 25 came around 6 a.m., with sunrise following about 6:30. Neither time triggered an immediate Federal assault. Instead, Sherman used the morning's semidarkness to reconnoiter. Since Sherman and his commanders had put their men to work fortifying overnight, the Union boys were weary and far from ready.

After 7:00 a.m., Sherman finally sent forward his first effort, more of a tap than a hammer-blow. Furthermore, his orders created confusion. Sherman reported that "General [John M.] Corse, with as much of his brigade as could operate along the narrow ridge, was to attack from our right center. General [Joseph A. J.] Lightburn was to dispatch a good regiment . . . to cooperate with General Corse." Corse's command numbered 900 rifles. Lightburn's "good regiment," the 30th Ohio, counted only 170 present, augmented by thirty men from the 4th West Virginia to total 200 troops. While other brigades were supposed to move along the base of the ridge in support, Sherman initially

A modern view of the entrance to the Sherman Reservation at Chattanooga and the trail up to the crest of Tunnel Hill. (dp)

sent only 1,100 men forward to try to seize the key point of the field—Tunnel Hill.

Lightburn, atop Billy Goat Hill, reported only that he received orders to send forward 200 men to "occupy Tunnel Hill," making no mention of Corse at all. In a postwar letter, Col. Theodore Jones of the 30th Ohio recalled that "Sherman was present and gave me these instructions: 'I wish you to go up the point of the hill and assist Corse who is coming up the side, and the sooner you get off the better as Corse is ready to start.'"

Sherman further muddied the waters when discussing affairs with Corse's divisional commander, General Ewing. "Ewing might go up [Tunnel] Hill 'if you like—if you can,' but, Sherman warned, 'don't call for help until you actually need it.'" This odd caution produced an equally strange order from Ewing to Col. John Loomis, whose brigade supported

Corse's flank at the foot of Missionary Ridge. Ewing instructed Loomis to "push the enemy's skirmishers [from the base of Missionary Ridge] but under no circumstances . . . bring on a general engagement." Considering Grant's orders to Sherman, this last curious injunction would likely leave Corse's men unsupported.

One more factor complicated the Union plan: the Confederates had moved. As the light faded on November 24, Cleburne's line extended the length of Tunnel Hill, facing west, the troops beginning to dig in. Both Cleburne and Hardee worried about being flanked, however, and before dawn, Cleburne ordered Brig. Gen. James A. Smith's Texans to shift position. Their new line anchored on the southern crest—the highest point—of Tunnel Hill and then ran eastward to connect with the rest of Cleburne's division on hills to the east. Even after dawn, the ground fog remained dense enough to obscure this new development from the observing Federals, meaning both Jones and Corse initially oriented to attack a Rebel line no longer there.

Mindful of Sherman's advice that Corse wait to begin, Colonel Jones led his mixed force of Ohioans and West Virginians up the northeast face of Tunnel Hill, deployed in a heavy skirmish line. They made contact right away with James Smith's Texans, also deployed as skirmishers on the lower slopes of Billy Goat Hill. With stronger numbers prevailing, Jones pushed the Texans slowly down that slope, across the intervening valley, and up the lower slopes of their objective, "striking the enemy's line of works in their rear and right flank . . . they were soon driven out and the works were ours." These works were not the main Confederate breastworks but instead the abandoned line the Texans now used as cover for their skirmishers. Still, Jones thought the capture significant. From these breastworks, he viewed a much stronger enemy position on the far crest,

perhaps 250 yards distant: earthen defenses manned by the 7th Texas and the four Napoleons of Swett's Mississippi Battery, commanded by Lt. Harvey Shannon.

Jones tried to organize a charge but lacked the numbers to challenge Cleburne's main line. After one brief sortie, he ordered the 30th to fall back to the abandoned works. From there, Jones later wrote, "I sent my Adjutant down the side of the hill from which I expected [General] Corse to come. After going some distance he returned with no tidings . . . ." Now, "somewhat alarmed," Jones "sent to Gen. Lightburn for reinforcements."

Jones clung to his toehold on Tunnel Hill for another hour before help arrived. Lightburn sent forward the 37th Ohio Regiment, which arrived about the same time Corse's forward elements appeared. That morning, Corse had formed his men with care, deploying into three skirmish lines and a reserve, consisting of the 6th Iowa and 103rd Illinois, which he placed under command of Col. Charles C. Walcutt of the 46th Ohio. Once ready, Corse ordered a cautious advance up the northern slope of Tunnel Hill. His van, five companies of the 40th Illinois commanded

This view shows the west end of the tunnel in Missionary Ridge, the view Union troops would have seen as they advanced. Although the Yankees believed that Confederates used the tunnel to sneak up on their flank, no Confederate report or account claims to have done so. (mcc)

The northern end of Missionary Ridge, viewed from the west, taken in 1864. (loc)

by Maj. Hiram Hall, did not step off until after 8:00 a.m. Soon thereafter, Sgt. E. J. Hart of Company E, regimental historian, noted, "the roar of musketry and artillery gave notice of a severe engagement" marking Colonel Jones's contact. Hall reached Jones's position at 9:00 a.m. or after.

With even fewer numbers than Jones, Hall nevertheless hazarded his own charge, also directed at Shannon's cannon. They initially overran the same abandoned line seized earlier by Jones's Ohioans—"two companies scaling the enemies outer works," noted Hart—but stopped short of the main line. Hall then ordered the 40th to fall back "a few rods down the hill" where they waited for Corse and the rest of the brigade.

When Corse arrived, he discovered the changed circumstances. After conferring with both Hall and Jones, Corse organized a new assault. Corse wanted Jones to shift "to the left and let his men in on the right," then all would charge straight for the redoubt. Jones protested, arguing that the Union line would have to make "a right wheel" and his men "would be under a crossfire as soon as they left the works." As if swayed, Corse ordered Colonel Jones to go find Sherman and request reinforcements.

To this point in the morning, Sherman had remained relatively inactive, observing the action from Billy Goat Hill. Sometime around 8:00 a.m., he sent word to Grant asking for support, a request which, at 9:45 a.m., produced an order from Grant to Howard instructing the XI Corps to "march to join Sherman." Somewhat reassured, Sherman refused an offer from Thomas of an additional division under Brig. Gen. Absalom Baird, saying, as one correspondent later related, "that he could do his work alone." Certainly, with the addition of Howard, Sherman had ample force at hand: 30,000 or more men.

Still, Sherman knew Grant expected results, and so far, none had developed. By 10:00 a.m., when Colonel Jones returned to Billy Goat Hill to relay Corse's request for support, Sherman revealed considerable agitation. "'Go back and make that charge immediately; time is everything,' [Sherman] snarled. 'If you want more men, I will give you all you want; if you want artillery, I will give you that. General Grant is on Orchard Knob waiting for your assault in order to send up a column from the Army of the Cumberland.'"

Colonel Jones hurried back to Corse and conveyed Sherman's instructions: immediate assault. In addition, Jones's mission produced a substantial Union artillery barrage, directed at softening up the Rebels atop Tunnel Hill before the charge, but they could not wait for reinforcements. Though Jones did not mention it, Sherman instructed Ewing to send orders to Col. John Loomis, whose brigade was operating against Missionary's western face, to make a simultaneous attack in support of Corse's effort. Given the terrain and distance between Loomis and Corse, however, such coordination would prove problematic.

Dutifully, Corse's infantry attack jumped off about 11:00 a.m. Corse's men advanced with a will, reaching the crest of Tunnel Hill, but then went no farther. The first three lines all fell back with loss. "His front rank is mowed down at one fell swoop," exulted Texas Sgt. Albert Jernigan, defending the hill. Badly disordered, the Federals stumbled back to the north crest, seeking shelter. Over on the Union left, Jones's Ohioans were further discomfited by fire coming in from the flank and rear: infantry musketry from Lowrey's Confederates on the next ridge east, several hundred yards behind them, and enfilading shell and canister from Douglas's Texas Battery to the south. With the Federals faltering, Confederate James Smith sensed an opportunity and lashed out a counterattack. Here, the Texans found some of those mowed-down Yankees only feigning death and promptly took them prisoner. Now, Union troops took a turn peppering their foe. Both Smith and Col. Roger Q. Mills of the combined 6th/10th/15th Texas fell, wounded. Colonel Hiram Granbury assumed command, pulling the Texans back into their defenses.

Next, Corse brought up the unengaged 6th Iowa and 103rd Illinois. He also shifted three companies each from the 40th and 103rd Illinois to the right, hoping to strike the Rebel line where it curved away to face west while the rest of Walcutt's reserve line charged directly through the remainder of the 40th Illinois men and the Buckeyes of the 46th Ohio, still recovering from that first effort of the day's fight. "Here they come again . . ." wrote Texas Capt. Samuel Foster, delighted at the prospect of another easy slaughter, "like they are going to walk right over us—Now we give them fits. . . . Oh this is fun to lie here and shoot them down and we not get hurt."

In this last, Foster's memory failed him. The Rebels took casualties, getting badly hurt. Swett's Mississippi Battery, supporting Smith's brigade, suffered so heavily that the depleted gun crews had to be augmented by details of infantrymen, and a corporal commanded the battery for a time. Cleburne brought up Key's Arkansas Battery and the combined 2nd/15th/24th Arkansas infantry to strengthen the Texans' hold on the hill.

Still, the Yankees suffered far heavier losses. General Corse left the field among the fallen, his leg badly contused by a shell fragment. Though the injury looked superficial, he remained out of action, bedridden, for several months. Command fell to Colonel Walcutt of the 46th Ohio, who attempted a new attack. That effort also failed.

Corse's repulse left Sherman feeling even less confident. At 12:45 p.m., he evidenced uncertainty in a plaintive three-word message to Grant: "Where is Thomas?"

Sherman Tries Again

CHAPTER SIX

NOVEMBER 25, 1863—MIDDAY

Colonel John Loomis and his brigade of Yankees, sent by General Ewing to operate at the base of Missionary Ridge and theoretically in support of Corse's flank, had been almost forgotten in the morning's action. Given Ewing's counter-intuitive instructions "not to bring on a general engagement," it should not be surprising that Loomis's four regiments accomplished little that morning. Captain Ira Bloomfield of the 26th Illinois remembered his regiment moving out on the right of Loomis's brigade line sometime after 8:00 a.m. "There was about 1200 men in line," he recollected. "We advanced until we reached the earth work made by constructions of the railroad track, and there was halted and were [laid] down for several hours under fire of sharpshooters."

Those Confederate sharpshooters belonged to Brig. Gen. John C. Brown's brigade, Stevenson's division, newly arrived and deployed to extend Cleburne's flank. Mindful of Ewing, Loomis made no effort to advance, though he did employ a section of Union artillery to try to silence Brown's skirmishers.

At 10:30 a.m., Loomis received "notice from Brigadier General Ewing that . . . Corse was

Another view of Tunnel Hill, from just behind the Confederate artillery and showing J. A. Smith's brigade tablet. The spire in the distance is the Iowa Monument. (hs)

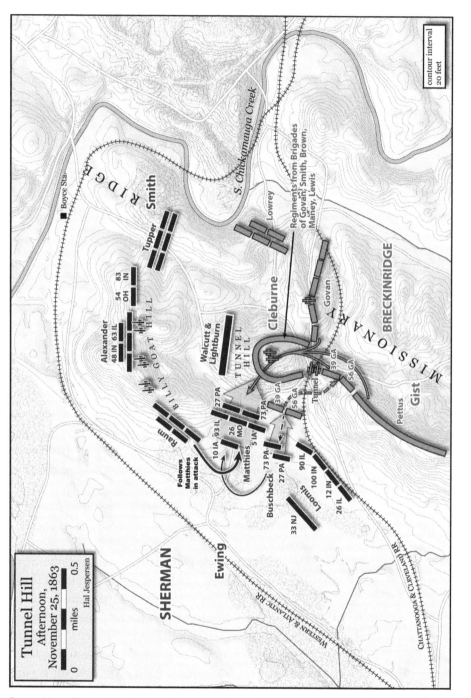

TUNNEL HILL—Sherman's subsequent attacks on Tunnel Hill were no more coordinated or effective than the morning phase, producing nothing but additional casualties.

about to assault Tunnel Hill, accompanied with an order to advance simultaneously. The order was promptly obeyed." This attack produced the single highest casualty total of any of Sherman's brigades but accomplished nothing. Loomis never came near reaching the crest of Tunnel Hill, let alone taking it. Instead, Loomis, who at the western foot of the ridge had no contact with Corse's line, moved southerly toward the mouth of the Tunnel and the Glass farm, which lay just below.

John M. Loomis went to sea as a teenager, sailing to India and China before entering the lumber business in Wisconsin. By 1861, he was a prominent Chicago businessman and raised the 26th Illinois infantry for war service. (ejs)

Totally exposed, the brigade line suffered severely. Captain Buck of Cleburne's staff recalled that the Federal line "approached Cleburne's left front, through an open field under heavy fire of artillery and musketry. [Lieutenant Thomas J. Key's] Napoleon guns, posted over the tunnels, and rapidly served, were turned upon this brigade with deadly precision. Every discharge plowed huge gaps through the lines . . . ." Irish-born Col. Timothy J. O'Meara of the 90th Illinois fell, the first of numerous Federal regimental commanders lost on this part of the field. Loomis's line halted at "an old fence row," south of the Glass farmstead and west of the rail line as it entered the tunnel, leaving a sizeable gap of several hundred yards between Loomis's 90th Illinois (the Chicago Irish Legion) on the brigade left and the rest of Sherman's forces arrayed against Tunnel Hill. Loomis, already worried about the gap, grew further concerned when skirmishers from Brown's Tennessee brigade threatened to turn Loomis's left. Brown reported that his skirmishers became "so hotly" engaged that "I reinforced the line [with] . . . nearly half my command."

Irish-born Col. Timothy O'Meara was killed in the assault on Tunnel Hill. Formerly of New York, O'Meara was hand picked by Chicago's Irish immigrant community to command the newly raised 90th Illinois Infantry. (alpl)

Confederate General Hardee also took a hand. Brown's brigade, a small one, still waited for one of its regiments (the combined 18th/26th Tennessee) to arrive. Accordingly, Hardee ordered Brig. Gen. Alfred Cumming, also of

This sketch of Loomis's brigade at Missionary Ridge shows Tunnel Hill to the left, the burning Glass farm in the center, and the railroad embankment with a line of skirmishers, angling from the right. (ejs)

Stevenson's division, to secure the Glass farm with two regiments, thereby threatening Loomis's left. Cumming chose the 39th and 56th Georgia for this task, hurrying them over from Brown's brigade left to the Tennesseans' right. Robert F. Magill of the 39th Georgia noted at "11 a.m. five companies . . . [were] thrown forward as skirmishers. [We] drove the yanks back from dwelling; ordered to fall back and did so, but in [a] few minutes were ordered to charge and go to the house, which was done, and the house set on fire. Soon after the family made their appearance, having been in the cellar."

It mattered little whether the house first caught fire from Union artillery engaging Brown's and Cumming's men or on Georgian orders. The blaze flushed out a handful of frightened women and children from the relative safety of their cellar into the middle of a firefight. The terrified civilians fled west, passing through the ranks of the 26th and 90th Illinois: "three frightened women, a few children and three yelping dogs." J. B. Bruner of the 26th remembered "a woman and a child came and passed through our lines—I think unhurt."

Loomis, pinned down, suffering severely, and now in danger of being flanked, ordered

up support. Into the gap on Loomis's left came Colonel Bushbeck, with his detached brigade of XI Corps men. Bushbeck commanded three regiments: the veteran 27th and 73rd Pennsylvania and the brand-new 33rd New Jersey, which had only mustered into service on September 3. The Jerseymen had never seen combat and came into the army with a reputation of being draft-dodgers and bounty jumpers. Though the 33rd would go on to perform well in future actions, now Bushbeck decided to send them to support Loomis, leaving him only two regiments to engage the main Rebel line.

Each Union attack was preceded by a skirmish line much like this one, sketched by Adolph Metzner of the 32nd Indiana, part of August Willich's brigade in Thomas Wood's division of the Union IV Corps. (loc)

Advancing in skirmish order, the 73rd Pennsylvania cleared the Glass farm complex, driving back the last of the Georgians. The 27th followed. Both regiments took some shelter behind hastily erected breastworks put together by the Rebels and now abandoned, but the safety did not last long. Bushbeck sent two companies of the 27th to extend the 73rd's left, an order that was subsequently misinterpreted by Maj. P. A. McAloon of the 27th as an order to storm the ridge. The entire regiment, "two hundred and forty strong," plus a company of the 73rd which joined in, surged up Tunnel Hill toward Key's Battery.

The Keystoners closed to within twenty

Georgian Alfred Cumming was a West Pointer, class of 1849, and a brigade commander at Vicksburg. He led his brigade in the Army of Tennessee until he was wounded at Jonesboro, September 1, 1864. (phcw)

yards, but no farther. The 27th halted, pinned down, exchanging enough fire to suppress Key's Arkansan gunners. The bulk of the 73rd's line remained near the Glass farm, clustered along a fence line at the foot of the ridge, sheltering to avoid being slaughtered and not willing to expose themselves in a retreat. Both Major McAloon of the 27th and Lt. Col. Joseph B. Taft of the 143rd New York—who had been temporarily assigned to command the 73rd due to that regiment's shortage of field officers—went down with wounds. Taft's mortal wounding occurred as he started for the rear to fetch more ammunition. Taft's last words ordered his unit to "hold this position at all hazards."

Bushbeck's foundered assault brought Loomis no relief. The Illinoisan could clearly observe movement within the Confederate lines, shifting troops northward, and Loomis interpreted it as a new effort to threaten his left flank. In reality, these troops moved to help Cleburne. Around 1:00 p.m., Brig. Gen. Alfred Cumming received an order to send a regiment to Cleburne. He dispatched the 39th Georgia, with the men's cartridge boxes newly replenished after their foray down to the Glass cabin. Immediately afterwards, Hardee requested a second regiment, and Cumming sent the 34th Georgia. Both regiments engaged hotly, supporting Key's battery where, noted Georgian Robert Magill, "Colonel [Joseph T.] McConnell [was] shot through the head, mortally wounded." McConnell, in peacetime a lawyer and Georgia State Representative from nearby Ringgold, would die six days later at home, just fifteen miles from where he fell. The fight for Tunnel Hill proved costly for regimental commanders on both sides.

Stymied, both Loomis and Bushbeck now looked for additional support. Two more Union brigades entered the fight, although in the same discordant manner as the previous units.

Colonel Green B. Raum's and Brig. Gen. Charles L. Matthies's brigades both belonged to John E. Smith's 2nd Division of the XVII Corps, though, to Smith's frustration, neither would fight under his immediate direction that day. Smith had been ordered to loan out both brigades to Hugh Ewing, commander of both Corse's and Loomis's commands. Smith received the first inkling things might not be going well when he rode forward to observe the action and found Raum's men standing, exposed, "about 20 paces in front of General Ewing's . . . entrenchments. . . . I at once called upon General Ewing for an explanation," Smith later reported, only to have Sherman himself override Smith's objections.

At about the time Bushbeck assailed Tunnel Hill, Ewing ordered Matthies's four regiments forward to "take that white house [the Glass farm]." Matthies complied, deploying his line alongside Loomis's left and coming into position behind Bushbeck. Lieutenant Mahlon Head of the 10th Iowa described that advance: "We ployed into line and moved forward under heavy fire . . . and took our position at the house as ordered. Lost some men killed and wounded by shells in charge & while lying at the house." Here, Head continued,

The crest of Tunnel Hill, studded with Rebel artillery, presented an ominous site to Union troops in their repeated assaults on that position. (dp)

"the house & out Buildings caught fire and the family and negroes . . . were compelled to come out and run to our rear for life . . . ."

While halted at the base of the ridge, Col. Holden Putnam of the 93rd Illinois approached Matthies, informing the brigadier that the 27th Pennsylvania was pinned down on the slope above and calling for help. Putnam wanted to move up; Matthies acquiesced.

"We charged up the peak," noted one of the 93rd, and "when we got to the top we was all almost exhausted . . . we lay down for a few minutes then advanced up within 15 steps of the enemy's works [and] found the 27th Penn there engaged . . . the roar of muskets was incessant . . . men was falling on every side of me . . . we hadn't been there 15 minutes till the center gave way but the officers succeeded in rallying them again. The Col. took the colors on his horse and waved them, telling the boys never to forsake them and at that moment he was shot dead . . . the ball penetrating his brain."

The 93rd now went alongside the Keystoners, stubbornly clinging to the small bit of defilade that allowed them to remain so close to the Rebel line. Matthies quickly dispatched an aide to report his position, and when that officer returned with word that another brigade was coming forward, Matthies ordered the rest of his brigade to move up and support the beleaguered 93rd Illinois. As he reached the forward line, just turning to caution the men "to fire low and sure," Mathies was "struck by a bullet in the head." When he regained consciousness, Matthies turned the command over to Col. Benjamin D. Dean of the 26th Missouri and made his way haltingly to the rear. Commanding officers suffered high casualty rates in the fight for Tunnel Hill.

As the morning drew on, Sherman seemed increasingly hesitant, even fearful, about the outcome of this engagement. Even though two-

Oliver O. Howard's XI Corps troops barely got into the fight for Tunnel Hill. Only Bushbeck's brigade saw any action. Sherman seemed to forget Howard's presence entirely when he asked, "Where is Thomas?" (loc)

thirds of his command had yet to see any action, and despite Howard's 10:00 a.m. reinforcements, Sherman looked for more help. At 12:45 p.m., he sent a plaintive message to Grant: "Where is Thomas?"

In the meantime, Colonel Raum's brigade now went forward. Raum observed the morning's fight with great interest. When Generals Ewing and John Smith came to him at about 2:00 p.m. to order him forward, the Colonel "replied that I had felt for some time that Matthies needed help." Formed in two lines, Raum sent his four regiments at the double-quick across the open valley to the foot of the ridge, where they took shelter in the wagon road at the base and prepared to charge up the slope. Here, Raum met Matthies coming down the hill, head bloody, who informed him about Colonel Putnam's fall and that the Federal ammunition at the top was nearly gone. Raum ordered his own line to charge up and through Matthies's men to take their places at the front.

So far, Cleburne's and Stevenson's men blunted every thrust of the Union's disjointed, individual attacks. Now, as Raum's men began ascending the ridge, Cleburne orchestrated

This view of Missionary Ridge looks generally at the north end of the ridge, showing ground over which Loomis's men likely advanced. This view dates from the 1890s, before Chattanooga had grown up around the terrain, but as can be seen, much of the vegetation has returned. (loc)

another counterattack, abetted by additional reinforcements from General Hardee: Brig. Gen. George Maney's brigade of Tennesseans. To Cleburne's left, Brig. Gen. Alfred Cumming contributed two Georgia regiments. Nor would

the Texans be left out. With half a dozen regiments, Cleburne's sudden counterstroke fell like a hammer blow.

With the combined 1st/27th Tennessee of Maney's command spearheading the charge, Cleburne's men suddenly surged out of their works and across the short distance—"fifteen paces" according to a postwar Tennessee account—"and in less than two seconds found themselves in the very midst of the Federals." The charge came at a terrible time. Matthies's men and the 27th Pennsylvania, desperately low on ammunition and with many senior officers down, were unprepared, and Raum's soldiers still toiled up the slope.

Col. Holden Putnam of the 93rd Illinois Infantry (above) led his regiment up this slope, where the monument can be found today (top). Putnam, mounted, was carrying his regiment's colors when he was mortally wounded. (hs)(hntri)

On the Union right, the 36th and 56th Georgia simultaneously tore into the flank of the 5th Iowa, stretched in a skirmish line on the Keystoners' right flank. "[We were] ordered to charge over our own breastworks," wrote Sgt. John E. Jeffares of the 36th, "which we did and routed the enemy and throwed them into utter confusion and disorder down the hill. . . . Such a slaughter I have never seen. The Yankees fell thick before us." The Iowans lost 82 men captured, from 227 taken into action, including their entire color guard.

The 93rd Illinois and 27th Pennsylvania now fled down the hill, right into and through Raum's relief line. Close on their heels came Rebels, from both front and flank; Raum's regiments could not hold. Many Federals later believed (and reported) some Confederates used the railroad tunnel to sneak around the Union flank, but in reality a convenient ravine provided ample cover. Raum, "in the midst of the Third [Matthies's] brigade and 17th Iowa," felt that "this front attack could . . . have been resisted, . . . but the movement upon our right flank was so sudden . . . that there was no time to make a change of front to meet it." Raum tried momentarily to rally the broken line but without success. He then fell back to the foot of the hill, chasing his retreating men and staying ahead of his pursuers. Reaching the road where his 56th Illinois and 10th Iowa stood in reserve, Raum recalled that "as I jumped down into the road, with a loud voice, I shouted, Fire!"

That fire checked Cleburne's pursuers about the time the Confederate general prepared to recall them anyway. His attack was successful, clearing the ridge and sweeping the Federals back down to the low ground. Cleburne reported captures of 500 men and eight sets of colors during the day's fighting, all at a cost of less than 250 casualties.

Sherman's appetite for assault, never very strong, was now thoroughly sated. Even though the bulk of his command had yet to see serious action, the Ohioan's thoughts now turned to defense. Fearing a larger counterattack, Sherman ordered Howard's reinforcements to strengthen Sherman's right along South Chickamauga Creek. As for the rest, Sherman sent word to Grant that he was digging in. Around 4:30 p.m., he received a shocking message in return. "Thomas has carried the hill . . . in his immediate front. Now is your time to attack with vigor. Do so."

Storming the Ridge

CHAPTER SEVEN

NOVEMBER 25, 1863—LATE AFTERNOON

Throughout the day, Sherman's lack of progress eroded Grant's equanimity. Initially, Grant took the lack of combat on Sherman's front as a sign that Bragg had indeed withdrawn, not just from Lookout, but from Missionary Ridge as well. At 7:30 a.m., Assistant Secretary of War Charles Dana telegraphed Washington, explaining the lack of "firing at [the] front . . . makes it pretty certain Bragg retreated." It wasn't until 9:00 a.m. that Dana amended his report to note that while "Bragg evacuated . . . Lookout Mountain last night . . . he still holds to his rifle pits along [the] base [of] Missionary Ridge . . . and has been moving troops . . . toward [the] front of Sherman's position."

These movements, coupled with Sherman's initial probe, triggered new orders. The first went to Howard's command at 9:45; General Baird received the second a short while later. Both commands were instructed to reinforce Sherman. Sometime after, Sherman decided he did not need Baird. Baird's large division of the XIV Corps began the morning on Thomas's right, linking with Hooker's men; the morning's aborted movement shifted them to Thomas's left, just north of Orchard Knob.

A modern view of the Illinois Monument at the Bragg Reservation, viewed from the west, as a Federal attacker would approach the ridge. (dp)

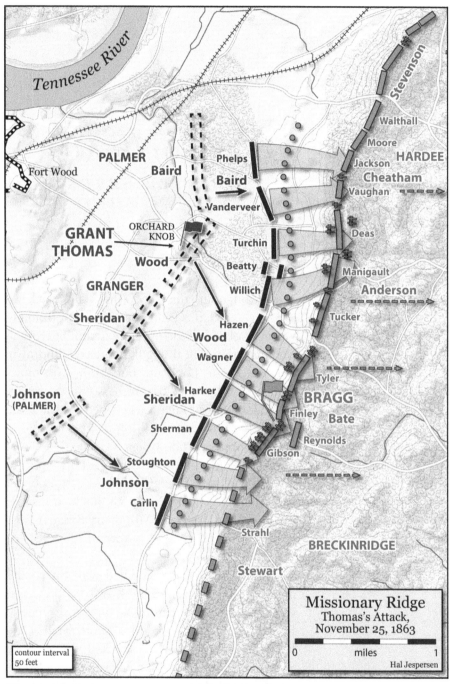

Tennessee River

Fort Wood

PALMER

Baird

Phelps

Baird

Vanderveer

Walthall

Moore

Jackson

HARDEE

Cheatham

Vaughan

GRANT

THOMAS

ORCHARD
KNOB

Wood

Turchin

Beatty

Deas

GRANGER

Willich

Manigault

Anderson

Sheridan

Hazen

Wood

Wagner

Tucker

Johnson
(PALMER)

Harker

Sheridan

Sherman

Tyler

BRAGG

Finley   Bate

Stoughton

Johnson

Carlin

Gibson

Reynolds

Strahl

BRECKINRIDGE

Stewart

Missionary Ridge
Thomas's Attack,
November 25, 1863

contour interval
50 feet

0   miles   1

Hal Jespersen

Missionary Ridge, Thomas's Attack—At 4:00 p.m., with Sherman's attacks stalled, Grant ordered George Thomas to move against the rifle pits at the base of Missionary Ridge. Four divisions of Federals took the pits, but then kept on going, storming the heights.

The other major change to Grant's plans involved Hooker. Grant's pre-dawn intentions for Hooker gave vague directions, largely contingent on the Rebels' actions. Hooker's main mission that morning focused on advancing around the east end of Lookout Mountain to seize Summertown Road—the Confederates' main access to and from the mountain's crest. If they still held the crest, they would then be trapped; if not, then the mountain could be occupied by Union forces. Very shortly after dawn, with the national flag planted on the crest, Hooker reported the crest secure and that "prisoners think they [the Rebels] have abandoned [Lookout] valley entirely. [I] have ordered a reconnaissance . . . and will know more presently."

Maj. Gen. Gordon Granger served as a divisional and corps commander under William S. Rosecrans before being given command of the Union IV Corps after the Army of the Cumberland was reorganized in October. Grant was unimpressed with Granger's performance during the Chattanooga campaign. (loc)

At 7:00 a.m., Thomas replied, instructing Hooker to "move forward immediately, in accordance with the instructions of last evening." Hooker complied, reporting by 9:20 a.m. that he had secured Lookout and Summertown Road. "I await orders," he sent. New instructions came fifty minutes later, at 10:10 a.m. Excepting two regiments, Hooker was to "move on the Rossville Road toward Missionary Ridge."

Grant joined Thomas at Orchard Knob sometime after 10:00 a.m. By then, the Knob bustled with activity; in addition to Grant's and Thomas's presence, corps commanders Gordon Granger and John M. Palmer made the place their headquarters as well. And why not? The view was superb. Newspaper correspondent Sylvanus Cadwallader later recalled that from this vantage, "the day and the ground conspired to give us an unbroken view of the whole field." From there, Grant witnessed Sherman's first major effort to take Tunnel Hill around midday and Baird's movement into position. The assembled officers also clearly saw Sherman's difficulties. Later, as they watched Sherman's second repulse, Cadwallader wrote that Grant "dropped his

A turn-of-the-century view of Bragg's headquarters site on Missionary Ridge, viewed from the north. You can see the Illinois monument just behind the War Department Viewing tower erected in the 1890s. Contrast this view with other, more modern views of the Bragg Reservation on pages 16, 62, and 122. (loc)

glass, turned to me, and said: 'Driving our boys quite lively, aren't they?' 'Yes, driving them back badly,'" replied the journalist. Grant appeared unruffled. Pointing out Sherman's headquarters flag, Grant said, "that's where Sherman is posted; he'll soon make it all right." As it turned out, the general's optimism proved unfounded.

The Union commander responded with less forgiveness toward Hooker. Although initially Hooker's column made good time, Chattanooga Creek's rapid, high-banked torrent stymied the advance by noontime. Also, while the Confederate retreat had been hasty, Carter Stevenson's soldiers had taken time to burn the creek's bridges, which Hooker's men would now have to rebuild. That task consumed the next several hours. Grant— and various of his supporters—later condemned Hooker harshly for this delay.

By nature, Grant was a reserved, taciturn man. Though to Cadwallader he might appear unruffled at Sherman's setbacks, Col. James A. Wilson, one of Grant's aides, remembered things differently. "At first everything seemed hopeful," recalled Wilson, "but as the day wore on . . . with nothing being done, the situation became exceedingly embarrassing. [Brig. Gen. John] Rawlins [Grant's chief of staff], always an anxious and questioning observer, grew sullen and finally indignant, first at Granger and next at Thomas himself. . . . Grant seemed anxious but undecided, and gave no positive orders . . . ."

Shortly after Sherman's plaintive 12:45 p.m. message asking about Thomas arrived, "Grant . . . modestly asked Thomas

if he didn't think he should make a demonstration in Sherman's favor." Thomas, who easily matched Grant in taciturnity, "not regarding the question as an order, stood unresponsive and silent."

Neither George Thomas (above) nor Grant intended the attack against Missionary Ridge to be anything more than a demonstration, aimed at seizing the first line of Confederate entrenchments at the base of the ridge. (loc)

The tension on Orchard Knob must have been thick. Relations, never good between Grant's and Thomas's headquarters personnel, deteriorated. Grant's people regarded the Cumberlanders as slow, plodding, and timid. Gordon Granger's antics on the Knob did not help matters. Granger, who had served as an artilleryman pre-war, spent much of the time indulging himself by sighting and firing a three-inch ordnance rifle belonging to Capt. Lyman Bridges's Illinois Battery, instead of attending to his duties as commander of the IV Corps. Wilson, Rawlins, and Brig. Gen. William F. Smith grew increasingly vocal in their frustrations as the hours dragged and nothing seemed to be happening. Thomas did dispatch an order to Hooker at noon, instructing him to flank the first line of Rebel works. However, when

In this 1886 print, General Grant on Orchard Knob views the unauthorized assault up the slopes of Missionary Ridge. He, Thomas, and Granger stand atop the flat rock on the left-center of the print. (loc)

Hooker replied, at 1:30, stating it would be at least another hour before he could cross Chattanooga Creek, Thomas made no further reply.

Then came Sherman's final effort, his repulse clearly visible, as noted by Cadwallader. With some understatement, Col. Joseph S. Fullerton, one of Granger's staff officers, noted, "The battle as planned had not been won." Something more needed to be attempted. At 3:00 p.m., Grant turned to Brig. Gen. Thomas Wood, who was also present: "Sherman seems to be having a hard time. . . . I think we ought to do something to help him." "Whatever you order we will try to do," Wood said.

Earlier in the day, the assembled commanders all thought a frontal assault against Missionary Ridge even "if successful"—itself a highly doubtful prospect—could come "only . . . at a great and unnecessary cost of life." Accordingly, Grant suspended any idea of such an attack until Sherman and Hooker successfully enveloped Bragg's flanks. Now, Hooker paused to repair bridges, and Sherman had been repulsed. What was left? Grant reasoned that it might be possible to seize the first line of Rebel works below the ridge, especially since it looked like Bragg had been steadily weakening his center to reinforce Tunnel Hill all day. At 3:30 p.m., Grant ordered Thomas "to advance his whole line against the rifle trench at the foot of the ridge."

Four divisions would make the attack. From left to right they included Baird, only recently arrived on the left from his former position on the right, then Wood, Sheridan, and Johnson. Wood and Sheridan, in the center, belonged to Granger's IV Corps while the flanking divisions of Baird and Johnson belonged to the XIV Corps.

Although years later Fullerton reported that the "only order given was to move forward and take the rifle pits at the foot of the ridge," Grant's instruction later triggered decades of controversy. In his official report, Grant asserted that his intent all along was to have the men move up the ridge after the first Rebel line had been seized, but only after reforming the lines into proper assault columns for the ascent. Others stated Grant never intended anything more than a demonstration.

An 1885 print of the same scene titled *The Battle of Chattanooga*. This image is much simpler than the previous one, and merely shows Grant, mounted and alone, observing the attack. (loc)

Certainly, the men at the cutting edge could not agree. Thomas Wood reported that "our orders carried us no farther" than "the first line of intrenchments." Brigadier General August Willich, commanding a brigade of Wood's division, vaguely reported that "I understand since that the order was given to take only the rifle pits at the foot of the ridge," but at the time "I did not understand it so; I only understood the order to advance." When Maj. John McClenahan of the 15th Ohio, commanding Willich's skirmish

This image, published by the McCormick Reaper Company, shows the assault on Missionary Ridge from a northern point on the ridge, looking south. Documentation identifies it as a scene "from the Panorama Painting on exhibit in Chicago." (loc)

line, asked the jovially gruff German where his skirmishers should halt, "he replied, 'I don't know, at Hades I expect.'"

Another of Wood's brigadiers—William Hazen, on Willich's immediate right—wrote that he "received orders to move forward . . . and take possession of the enemy's works at the foot of Mission Ridge . . . there to await further orders"; these instructions sounded much like Grant's professed intent.

Absalom Baird had yet a different understanding. As historian Peter Cozzens described it, Baird was initially instructed to take just the first line, orders relayed by Brig. Gen. William F. "Baldy" Smith. "'And when I have captured the rifle pits, what then?' [Baird] asked. Smith shrugged. 'I have given you the order in the exact words of General Grant.' Smith rode away. A few minutes later, [James] Wilson arrived, bearing the same instructions . . . General Thomas, Wilson said, intended the advance to be 'preparatory to a general assault on the mountain, and that I [Baird] should take part in this movement, so that I would be following [Thomas's] wishes were I to push on to the summit.'"

General Philip Sheridan also doubted if he heard right. The orders he received from Granger seemed clear enough: "to carry the enemy's rifle pits at the base of Mission Ridge." In looking over the intended objective, however, Sheridan thought since "the first line of pits . . . would prove untenable after being carried, . . . the doubt arose in my mind whether I had properly understood the original order." Sheridan dispatched an aide to go find Granger and clarify. Before that officer returned, six evenly spaced cannon shots from Bridges's battery on Orchard Knob rang out. The signal to attack had sounded.

At first glance, the Confederate defenses appeared strong—perhaps impregnable. But several factors all contributed to create dangerous flaws in the Rebel position, including Confederate confusion over orders, confusion matching or exceeding Federal confusion.

First and foremost, Bragg's army lacked numbers. The troops seen moving by the Federals throughout the day were not hurrying to support Cleburne, rather they moved up to man the newly constructed defenses atop the ridge. Bragg certainly did commit his men disproportionately to the north end of the ridge; Hardee's four divisions all deployed north of army headquarters near the Moore house, leaving Breckinridge's three divisions to cover the remaining four miles of front to Rossville. Historian Larry Daniel noted only "two regiments and a battery" defended the Rossville Gap.

As for those Rebel defenses, the hastily constructed breastworks, most created in the dark, had only been partially completed. Most of the artillery—which should have been the backbone of Bragg's defense—was absent until recalled to the ridge on the morning of November 25, after Bragg's last-minute, overnight decision to stand firm. Bragg eventually committed ninety-six cannon atop the ridge (out of an army total of 145 guns) but many of them didn't get into position until only minutes before the Federal attack commenced. The crews of

This image is taken from a much larger picture, which in turn is one of a dozen photographs taken of another cyclorama of the battle of Missionary Ridge. This Panorama was painted in 1885 by a German company. It depicts Union troops assaulting the area of Bragg's headquarters—the house visible in upper background— and where the Illinois Monument sits today. (whs)

the Washington artillery, for example, reached their designated position only at 3:30 p.m., ten minutes before the Union signal guns touched off. "A number of batteries," noted Daniel, "lacked [any] protective earthworks."

The Confederates also struggled through the curious decision to try manning the defenses both at the base of the ridge and the new works at the crest. This order originated with Maj. Gen. John C. Breckinridge, whose corps now held the bulk of the ridge. To accomplish this, the Rebels split their forces again, leaving half their manpower at the foot and the other half at the crest. Divisional, brigade, and even in some cases regimental commanders tried to command formations divided between the bottom and the top of the ridge, separated by a steep slope. This command situation produced confusion and uncertainty. Some of the defenders at the base of the ridge thought they held at all costs, but many others thought they should only delay the Federals and then scramble up to the top. As a strategy, it was a recipe for disaster.

In fact, the Rebels had abandoned parts of their lower line before the Federals stepped off. In his post-war memoir, Brig. Gen. Arthur Manigault, whose brigade held the center of Brig. Gen. Patton Anderson's divisional line, explained that "the instructions to the officers in the lower line were . . . to await the approach of the enemy to within two hundred yards, deliver their fire, and then retire to their works above . . . ." Manigault regarded both the deployment and the orders as "most injudicious." Members of the brigade next in line to his left, however, understood things somewhat differently.

Colonel William F. Tucker commanded those troops, four regiments and a battalion of Mississippians. He reported that on the twenty-fifth, "one half the brigade [was] in one rank in the trenches & the other half busy engaging at the top of the Ridge." Around midday, Tucker noted, "orders were received that if the enemy advanced in force, the men at the foot of the ridge *were not to fight where they were*, but fall back skirmishing." As accounts from within the ranks of the 7th Mississippi Infantry make clear, however, that did not happen. Instead, "we rejoined our command at the top of Missionary Ridge about a half an hour before the general advance of the enemy," noted the commander of combined Companies E and K. Another member, writing home on December 2, explained that the men, exhausted from the climb, "were only able to rest for about thirty minutes when all eyes went to the plain below where five lines of battle were advancing."

At most, the advancing Federals met only light resistance from the Confederate lower line, and in some cases, no resistance at all. They captured the lower works with unexpected ease. Once there, however, things changed.

Sheridan's worries about holding at the foot of the ridge proved well grounded. Just to Sheridan's north, Brig. Gen. William Hazen's brigade of Wood's command experienced the validity of Sheridan's concern; the 41st Ohio regimental history describes their plight: "The Forty-first threw itself down against the logs for shelter, and the second line of troops . . . did the same. The [enemy] on the ridge opened a severe fire, and [their] artillery, by firing obliquely . . . was able to be effective. . . . No fight could be made from that insufficient . . . shelter. It was destruction to remain, it was impossible to withdraw without confusion and great loss."

Who was first to commence the charge up the slope? Who first crested the ridge? These questions provided debate long after the event. Probably Wood's Federals started first; Wood, among the men of his second line, watched his first ranks raggedly work their way up. "'General, we can carry the ridge!'" Wood looked around, and "said, 'Can you do it?' They said, 'We can.' 'Men, go ahead!'" Major McClenahan and his Union skirmishers, already a good ways up, watched in admiration: "Each regiment [advanced,] slightly V shaped, with the colors at the apex. . . . [As] soon as our line arrived we pushed on up."

On Wood's left, Brig. Gen. John Turchin's brigade spearheaded Baird's advance. Turchin, a native-born Russian, aggressively and liberally interpreted Baird's orders, pushing forward at once. Baird's other two brigades halted at the lower works, intending to reform first before scaling the ridge. Baird, hurrying in that direction, was shocked to receive new instructions: "Not to permit my men to go farther, and not to permit them to become engaged." This order might have heralded disaster, leaving Turchin to race up the ridge alone, except the contradiction arrived within "three minutes": disregard, go on up.

Grant, Thomas, Granger and their assembled staffs' consternation brought on that stutter-step as they watched from the front-row seat of Orchard Knob. A number of observers variously described this famous scene, which spawned decades of post-war debate. In 1866, journalist William Shanks remembered "Thomas turned to Grant and said, with a slight hesitation, which betrayed the emotions which raged within

This stark monument, a single upraised cannon, marks the spot where Lt. Col. Edward H. Phelps was killed at the crest of Missionary Ridge. Phelps, already wounded once during the ascent, refused to leave the field. Phelps was commanding the brigade at the time and was the only Union brigade-level commander killed or wounded during the engagement. (hs)

him, 'General, I—I'm afraid they won't get up.'" Grant, "continuing to look steadily" at the assaulting columns, "hesitated half a minute" and then, brushing away some cigar ash, replied, "Oh, give 'em time, general."

Joseph Fullerton, Granger's staff officer, recalled a much different (and more widely quoted) reaction. "I heard [Grant] say angrily, 'Thomas, who ordered those men up the ridge?' Thomas replied, in his usual slow, quiet manner, 'I don't know; I did not.'" Grant repeated his question to Granger. "'No,' said Granger; 'they started up without orders. When those fellows get started all hell can't stop them.'" Grant's only reply, according to Fullerton, was "something to the effect that somebody would suffer if it did not turn out well."

Granger dispatched couriers to find out what had happened, but the battle now raged beyond the generals' control. Like a ragged, rising tide, those arrowheads of troops followed their colors up the ridge in a dozen different places.

Confederate command confusion greatly aided the Union advance. On Sheridan's front, the orders received by Brig. Gen. Alexander Reynolds's mixed brigade of North Carolinians and Virginians amply demonstrated that confusion. Reynolds had 995 men in the ranks, split half on top and half below the ridge. Just before the Federal attack began, Reynolds received orders to bring the lower line to the crest. In order to avoid casualties from Federal artillery, he did so by companies, sending them up in skirmish order, which resulted in considerable scattering once at the crest, and caused some disruption among some of the other Confederate troops. This retreat removed all opposition from in front of Sheridan's left, but over on his right, an intermediate line of Tennesseans offered opposition halfway up the ridge.

Like Baird, Sheridan's advance was at first checked by order: Brig. Gen. George Wagner's brigade swarmed over the trenches just recently abandoned by Reynolds only to be halted by an order from Granger as they were starting to ascend the slope. Sheridan found them here. He conferred quickly with Granger's staffer, who told Sheridan that "if, in my judgment, the ridge could be taken, to do so." Up went Sheridan's men.

Colonel Francis Sherman's brigade, over on Sheridan's right, now had orders to carry that intermediate line of works. Undermanned, this second line fell within the space of about ten minutes, reported Sherman, whereupon the Yankees rested a few minutes before making their final lunge.

Confederate fire from the top of the ridge intensified, although in some sites the Rebels had trouble depressing their artillery sufficiently. Confederate General Reynolds reported that Patton Anderson, who was with him at the time, ordered "the guns to be depressed, & open on them with canister . . . so terrible was the effect . . . that it caused them to falter for an instant." Much of that fire, however, went high.

In the 24th Wisconsin, one of Sherman's leading regiments, the regiment's adjutant, Lt. Arthur McArthur, took the colors from the winded Color Sgt. John Borth, who at forty-four was one of the older men in the unit. The eighteen-year-old son of a Milwaukee judge dashed ahead with the colors for the final push. Years later, McArthur described the moment to his son, Douglas: "While I was carrying the flag a whole dose of canister went through it tearing it in a frightful manner." The projectiles flew high, though, and McArthur sustained only "one scratch . . . through the rim of my hat." McArthur and his flag reached the crest among the very first up the heights as part of a seemingly unstoppable flood of men in blue. McArthur was awarded the Congressional Medal of Honor for his determined actions. The citation stated that McArthur "seized the colors of his regiment at a critical moment and planted them on the captured works on the crest of Missionary Ridge."

To the chagrin of their officers, the Rebel defenders seemed seized by panic at the sight of all those Federals. Units and parts of units began to break rearward. The break, which probably began first among Colonel Tucker's Mississippians, soon spread. The Confederate defenders, already stretched thin—with regiments reduced to a single rank and the men three feet apart—fell back as Union numbers on the crest tipped the balance. The Mississippians' retreat allowed Wood's Yankees to gain the crest on

---

Manigault's southern flank, and then Manigault's men were gone.

Colonel Randall Gibson, leading a Louisiana brigade in A. P. Stewart's division, and Col. Jesse Finley's Florida brigade, both stationed near Bragg's headquarters, met Sheridan's men when they crested. Colonel William B. Bate's Tennessee brigade, led by Col. R. C. Tyler since Bate commanded the division, posted just to Finley's right. Bragg reported only Bate/Tyler's men on this portion of the line maintained any semblance of order. "A panic which I had never before witnessed," lamented Bragg, "seemed to have seized upon officers and men, and each seemed to be struggling for his personal safety, regardless of his duty or his character." Disaster overtook the Confederate army.

This view of Orchard Knob dates from about 1897, before many of the later monuments (including the large Illinois Monument) were erected. This view is from the east, as the Confederates would have seen the Knob. (pcc)

At one point, Bragg tried to personally stop the rout. When the color-bearer of the 3rd Florida fell, Bragg dismounted to seize the flag. Re-horsed, he rallied the regiment, until another Floridian took up the colors. "General Bragg was a brave old soldier, even if he was a tyrant to his men," marveled Lt. Henry Reddick of the combined 1st and 3rd Florida.

Bragg ordered Bate to reform and counterattack, but Bate protested the order as unworkable. It mattered little. Word shortly came that A. P. Stewart's division (next in line to the south) was giving way, having been flanked via the Rossville Gap. Sending instructions to both Hardee and Breckinridge to fall back to Chickamauga Station, beyond the banks of Chickamauga Creek, Bragg rode off in that direction himself, working his way through the mobs of retreating Rebels. Private Sam Watkins of the 1st Tennessee infantry recounted that as Bragg rode by, "the soldiers would yell . . . 'Bully for Bragg, he's hell on retreat.'" Now even Watkins, a confirmed Bragg-hater, admitted that "[I] felt sorry for him. Bragg looked so . . . hacked and whipped and mortified and chagrinned at defeat."

For the Federals, it was an astounding, astonishing victory. The fleeing Rebels abandoned dozens of artillery pieces, most of them only recently rushed into position on the heights. Flags and hundreds of prisoners were captured. It might have been worse for the Confederates, except for three things. First, growing darkness made it too late to organize a real Union pursuit. Second, the Rebels knew the roads and terrain on Missionary Ridge's eastern face intimately, but to the ridge's conquerors the ground represented— relatively speaking—*terra incognita*. Finally, the climb up the ridge's extreme western face under fire had exhausted and badly disorganized the Yankees. Sheridan organized a limited push by Harker's and Wagner's men, who chased a few Rebels down the backside of the ridge, but no one pushed far.

Tunnel Hill at the ridge's north end, still firmly held by Hardee's Corps, presented a matter still unsolved. Those Confederates won their fight and could not simply be ignored. The farther east the IV and XIV corps men pushed, chasing Bragg's collapsed center, the more they exposed their own left to a counterstroke from Hardee's determined veterans.

The Union right, though, rested free from such threats. Joe Hooker had taken Rossville.

The Fight at Rossville

CHAPTER EIGHT

NOVEMBER 25, 1863—MIDDAY TO DARK

On November 25, the men comprising General Joseph Hooker's mixed command awoke to a morning of uncertainty after spending a cold, uncomfortable night on the slopes of Lookout Mountain. Hooker's previous orders assumed the Confederates would continue to hold Lookout's summit and directed him to secure the Summertown Road, the road to the village of Summertown, located atop Lookout Mountain. Control of this road would isolate any Rebels still on the mountain from Bragg's main body on Missionary Ridge. Any lingering Confederates would be forced to retreat more than ten miles south, before they could descend the mountain's eastern face at Nickajack Gap.

However, as Hooker discovered by mid-morning, no Rebels remained. Hooker's composite column—including the 1st Division of the IV Corps, 2nd Division of the XII Corps, and Peter Osterhaus's 1st Division of the XV Corps, totaling about 12,000 troops—had no role to play in Grant's grand scheme. Action came, though, as already noted, shortly after 10:00 a.m. when Thomas directed Hooker to move eastward across Chattanooga Valley and capture Rossville.

The Rossville Gap was the most significant

Another Iowa Monument. This spire stands at the southern end of the Missionary Ridge battlefield, at Rossville, and is similar to the monument in the Sherman Reservation. (hs)

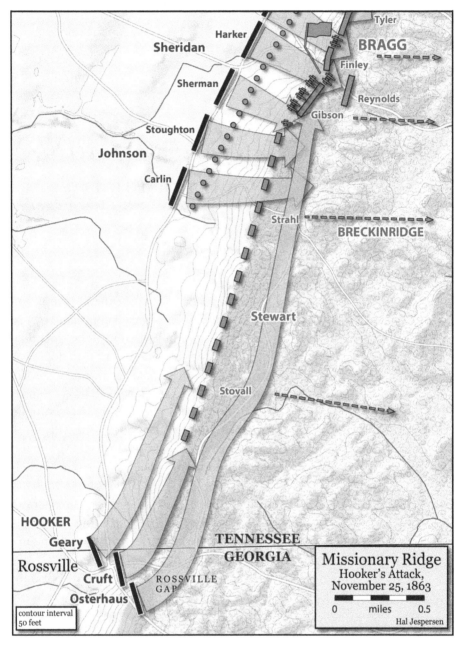

MISSIONARY RIDGE, HOOKER'S ATTACK—Joseph Hooker's attack against Rossville, which came almost as an afterthought, proved to be one of the most decisive strokes of the day. After securing the Rossville Gap, Hooker turned his three divisions northward, moving along the spine and both flanks of Missionary Ridge. Osterhaus, whose men penetrated all the way to the Bragg Reservation, completely enveloped Bragg's southern flank.

passage through Missionary Ridge. The Federal Road (which pre-dated the 1830's Cherokee removal) ran from Chattanooga through the gap to Ringgold and, ultimately, deep into Georgia. Control of the gap would turn Bragg's southern flank and open access to the Army of Tennessee's lifeline, the Western & Atlantic Railroad. Chickamauga Station was only a couple of miles east of Missionary Ridge, and Ringgold twelve miles to the southeast.

By the time Thomas's orders were received, Sherman's fight with Cleburne atop Tunnel Hill raged in full fury, easily observed from

Lookout's slopes, adding urgency to Hooker's new mission. Stepping off at around 10:30 a.m., Osterhaus's men led the march. Since no Union cavalry was available, a contingent of mounted infantry under command of Capt. W. T. House, serving as Osterhaus's headquarters escort, went forward to reconnoiter. Chattanooga Creek bisected Chattanooga Valley, flowing south to north and emptying into the Tennessee River at Moccasin Bend. In November 1863, the creek ran deep and fast from all the recent rains. House's scouts soon sent back both good news and bad: no Confederates waited west of the creek, but the bridges across that creek had all been burned. Hooker's column would be effectively stalled until a new bridge could be erected.

Shortly before noon Hooker's lead infantry regiment, the Union 27th Missouri, slipped across the creek on a footbridge improvised out of driftwood. Deployed as skirmishers, the

Union Maj. Gen. Joseph Hooker almost played no role in Grant's plans. Both the fighting at Lookout Mountain and at Rossville came largely as afterthoughts, dictated by last-minute circumstances. Grant expected Hooker to produce no great success. (loc)

Confederate Maj. Gen.
Alexander P. Stewart's
division was assigned to
defend the southern half
of Missionary Ridge, from
Bragg's headquarters to
Rossville Gap. His division
was stretched too thin to
defend the length of ridge
assigned him. (loc)

Missourians pushed eastward toward Rossville while Osterhaus's pioneer detachment went to work on a more substantial structure which would allow passage of artillery and ammunition wagons.

So far, Hooker's column had met scant opposition, uncovering instead "evidence of hastily abandoned camps, tents, bayonets, hospitals, and wounded," and there seemed to be only "two regiments and two guns" covering the train of wagons fleeing Hooker's approach, as recorded by Maj. Gen. Daniel Butterfield, Hooker's chief of staff. Repairing the bridge, however, imposed significant delay.

Early in the afternoon Hooker received additional instructions from Thomas, in a dispatch written at noon, providing additional tactical details: "I wish you [Hooker] and General Palmer to move forward firmly and steadily upon the enemy's works in front of Missionary Ridge, using General Sheridan as a pivot." At 1:25 p.m., Hooker answered, explaining that it would be some considerable time before he could execute those instructions: "I have been delayed preparing [the] crossing at Chattanooga Creek. . . . Shall be stopped perhaps an hour." That response reached Thomas at Orchard Knob near 2:00 p.m., adding to Grant's mounting frustration.

The 42nd and 43rd Georgia, totaling 600 strong and commanded by Col. Robert J. Henderson, opposed Osterhaus's 27th Missouri. These Confederates, detached from Brig. Gen. Marcellus Stovall's brigade of A. P. Stewart's division, had been sent to guard Rossville Gap. Unfortunately for Henderson, his nearest supports were far to the north.

Bragg had given Stewart's division a daunting task earlier on November 25: defend Missionary Ridge south from Bragg's headquarters all the way to Rossville, a distance of 2.3 miles. The division had no time to prepare earthworks or other defenses. Just 24 hours previously, Stewart's men had held the line across Chattanooga Valley, which had to be evacuated when Bragg abandoned Lookout Mountain. The other two divisions involved in that movement—Carter Stevenson's and John K. Jackson's—shifted to the Confederate right, supporting Hardee, where at least some of them fought Sherman. This decision left Stewart's men to defend the southern half of Missionary Ridge alone, a distance far too long for Stewart's four brigades to defend securely. Stewart instead concentrated most of his men on the north end of his sector. A mile wide gap existed between Henderson's detached Georgians and the next brigade to their north.

Colonel Henderson placed his Georgians about "300 yards" in front (west) of Rossville Gap, "on a slight eminence," supported by the four guns of Capt. Ruel Anderson's Georgia battery. Soon, the Georgians engaged with the Federal Missourians. Confederate reports place this initial encounter at various times, but mostly before noon. Captain Anderson estimated he opened fire at 10:30 a.m. Union reports, however, suggested times shortly after noon. In any case, the skirmishing, periodically intense, lasted about two hours.

Union Brig. Gen. Peter J. Osterhaus's division led Hooker's advance on Rossville Gap. Osterhaus was one of the more capable German-Americans who joined the Union armies. His troops, after moving through the gap, turned north and advanced as far as the modern-day Bragg Reservation. (loc)

Meanwhile, Osterhaus's infantry continued crossing the creek, either by fording or via the driftwood footbridge. Near 1:30 p.m., he pushed his two brigades forward to join the 27th Missouri in front of the gap, leaving his artillery and ordnance wagons behind in the process. The cannons and wagons moved with Geary's division for the rest of the day.

Once present, Osterhaus dispatched his brigades to scale the ridge on each of Henderson's flanks. Captain Anderson reported that he "discovered a heavy column of infantry . . . marching to my left. . . . I shelled it vigorously." These troops, Col. James Williamson's Iowans, comprised Osterhaus's 2nd Brigade. Colonel

The Ross house sits in Rossville Gap, giving that feature its name. John Ross, a mixed-heritage Cherokee chief, no longer lived in the house by the time of the Civil War; he had joined most of his tribe in the Cherokee Removal to what is now Oklahoma in 1838. This image dates from early 1864. (loc)

George Stone of the 25th Iowa acknowledged the accuracy of Anderson's fire. At 2:00 p.m., Stone noted, "We had just formed in line of battle . . . when the enemy's artillery became so annoying that we commenced to gain distance to the right [south]." Brigadier General Charles Woods's Federal brigade did the same to the north. Threatened with a double envelopment, Henderson "now ordered a retreat" to a piece of the ridge that overlooked the gap. Osterhaus pursued, and after another sharp fight, Henderson fell back again, leaving Rossville to the Federals.

Hooker's movement did not go unnoticed. Bragg observed it from his position atop Missionary Ridge and alerted Breckinridge to the threat.

Here, the Confederates made one of their most unfortunate command decisions of November 25. Breckinridge's corps held Bragg's center, and Breckinridge had earlier originated the poorly conceived idea to split his command between the foot and crest of the ridge. Now having seen Hooker's progress, Bragg conferred

with Breckinridge—who displayed a severely misguided confidence in the strength of the Confederate center, a sentiment with which Bragg so far seemed to agree. The commander ordered Breckinridge to conduct a "reconnaissance" south toward Rossville. Bragg took personal command of Breckinridge's line in the interim. Just before 3:00 p.m., the four Federal divisions below started to stir but had not yet begun their attack. The Confederate command confusion untimely stripped some units from the foot of the ridge before the Army of the Cumberland even advanced, probably during this transition from Breckinridge to Bragg.

Breckinridge appropriated Col. James Holtzclaw's Alabama brigade from Stewart and marched south along the spine of the ridge. He sent his son, Cabell Breckinridge, who served as an aide on his father's staff, ahead to coordinate with Colonel Henderson's Georgians.

Cabell Breckinridge found no Georgians. Instead, he stumbled into the ranks of the 9th Iowa, who promptly captured him. He was

This image of Rossville Gap was taken in 1864. It shows the appearance of the gap as Osterhaus's men would have seen it. After years of war, the area was largely denuded of trees. (loc)

This modern image of Rossville Gap shows roughly the same approach as the 1864 image. The trees have returned. The Iowa Monument sits in the middle of the gap. (dp)

brought to Osterhaus, whereupon the young man asserted that the Confederates "were winning the battle to that point"—true enough at the time. After appropriating young Breckinridge's fine white mare for his own use, Osterhaus sent the prisoner to the rear.

Hooker now had control of the gap and troops on the south end of Missionary Ridge. Thomas's

last instruction had been to join with Johnson to attack the Rebels at the western foot of the ridge, but Hooker expanded on that instruction. Leaving two regiments to guard Chattanooga Valley, Hooker ordered Osterhaus to deploy into line east of the crest, oriented north. Brigadier General Charles Cruft's two brigades from the IV Corps ascended to the spine, connecting with Osterhaus's left flank. Geary, with the column's artillery, took position on Cruft's left, to directly envelop the Confederate works along the base of the western face. Hooker intended all three divisions to then drive north, taking the entire Confederate position from the flank.

Meanwhile John Breckinridge led the Alabamans south, hoping to hear word from his son that Henderson still possessed Rossville. Three companies of skirmishers from the 36th Alabama led the column. The main body followed, marching "by the flank," (column of fours) due to the narrow crest. At roughly 4:00 p.m., those Alabamans met General Cruft, his

This closer image of Rossville Gap shows the rise of ground directly behind the Iowa Monument, where Confederate infantry and a battery were stationed during the initial phases of the engagement. (dp)

Brig. Gen. James T. Holtzclaw's Alabama brigade, of Stewart's division, was badly mauled as they moved south to try and contain the Union breakthrough along the south end of Missionary Ridge. (phcw)

mounted escort company and staff, as well as Col. William Grose with his staff, all conducting a reconnaissance of their own. The Rebels opened fire. Cruft's party fell back on the Federal main line, still toiling up the slope.

Drawn by the fire, Col. Isaac Suman led the 9th Indiana into a charge, scattering the Alabama skirmishers and forcing a hurried deployment by Holtzclaw's troops. Captain Benjamin L. Posey of the 38th Alabama remembered the extreme confusion. Posey, who doubled as the prolific correspondent for his hometown newspaper under the pseudonym "Ben Lane," voiced his dissatisfaction with Holtzclaw's choice to march "by the flank," which made it hard for the regiments to go into line. They were only able to manage it, noted Posey, "in some incomprehensible way." Suman's Hoosiers drove the Alabamans back some 300 yards, to a line of old defensive works (ironically, built by some of Cruft's Federals back in September) where the two sides settled in to exchange fire.

The confusion resulting from this encounter split Holtzclaw's brigade in two, with the rear half of the brigade deploying in an old field 400 yards farther north. This split left the Alabamans confronting Cruft in danger of breaking; even worse, Osterhaus's Federals moved north along the east slope in large numbers past Holtzclaw's left flank. For these reasons, as Captain Posey recorded with great dismay, the Confederate line began to unravel. Lieutenant Colonel John Inzer, commanding the combined 32nd/58th Alabama, was in that part of the brigade confronting Osterhaus. Inzer's first real inkling of trouble came when men of the 36th and 38th Alabama "came running out over us." Rushing to rally his own regiment before it, too, fled, Inzer "ran down the line, placed the colors, and attempted to form the line here." He was only partially successful. They held for a time—some

GEARY'S DIVISION—SLOCUM'S CORPS.
BRIG. GEN. JOHN W. GEARY.
NOV. 25, 1863, 6 P.M.
1ST BRIGADE — COL.
2ND BRIGADE — COL. WILLIAM R. CREIG
3RD BRIGA

participants said an hour; some said only twenty minutes—but Holtzclaw's men could not stop Hooker's entire wing.

Close to 5:00 p.m., George Thomas's IV and XIV corps men had crested the ridge all along the Confederate line, breaking Bragg's center and routing large portions of the Confederate army. Brigadier General Richard Johnson's division was the southernmost, and his right-flank brigade—Carlin's—was firmly astride the crest north of Holtzclaw's last position. The Alabamans were basically encircled. Retreating north and east, Inzer discovered this unpleasant reality when his men started surrendering to members of the Union 2nd Ohio Infantry. Inzer had no choice but to follow suit, and he spent the rest of the war in Union prison camps.

General Breckinridge barely escaped the same fate. By now the former vice president felt, in the words of one historian, "profoundly depressed." While making for safety, he stumbled upon A. P. Stewart, who described the moment: "He was

Though the Missionary Ridge neighborhood has attracted some of Chattanooga's most impressive homes, we can still appreciate the terrain the two armies faced. This view shows Union Brig. Gen. John W. Geary's divisional approach, taken from the top of the ridge looking southwest. Lookout Mountain can be seen in the distance. Geary's men would be approaching the camera head-on. (dp)

This, another of Adolph Metzner's drawings, depicts the 32nd Indiana cresting the ridge at the moment of victory and as the last of the Rebel defenders leave their positions. The Federals claimed the capture of more than 50 pieces of Confederate cannon, many of them re-captured Union guns lost at Chickamauga two months before. (loc)

in a great state of distress, and informed me that he had fallen into Hooker's column . . . [which] turned our flank—that [Holtzclaw's] brigade had been cut to pieces and captured, and he had lost his son." Bragg would later charge that Breckinridge was drunk. Although little contemporary evidence corroborates that accusation, there is no doubt that whatever the cause, Breckinridge's unfounded optimism on the night of the twenty-fourth, coupled with wildly erratic behavior during the twenty-fifth, contributed greatly to the Rebel disaster.

The Union troops won a great victory on November 25, their triumph cut short only by the fast-approaching darkness. Osterhaus later lamented that if the Federals had had only two more hours of daylight, Bragg's whole army might have been destroyed. In the end, Bragg's Confederates lost significant numbers: out of the roughly 44,000 engaged, the South suffered more than 6,600 casualties, 4,146 taken as prisoners, and roughly 3,000 of those were captured in the fighting on the twenty-fifth.

The Confederate lines in Bragg's center and left shattered, and the troops fled from the victorious Federals. Unable to contain himself, Grant, "determined to go to the summit," now left Orchard Knob, wrote Gen. Montgomery Meigs, to "see that proper order was restored." Meigs and other officers followed.

Atop the ridge, they found the wildest confusion. The command party crested Missionary Ridge in Baird's sector, and beyond Baird's left the Confederates still spoiled for a fight. These troops—Hardee's units who had repelled Sherman's repeated advances—showed little inclination to flee. Meigs struggled to get some of the captured Rebel cannon back into action, even using part of his own sword belt as a makeshift lanyard, and asked Grant to send back word to bring up trained gun crews. Then Meigs rode north with Baird, a moment he recorded the next day in his journal: "We spoke to every officer, [and] many men, wild with excitement—color bearers seeking their Colonels and men seeking their colors—urged the necessity of forming the men at once and that Bragg's army might by a charge sweep us from the ridge."

Grant embarked on a similar mission as he headed south. Mostly, he restrained additional pursuit, trying instead to restore order and command to the Federal troops. Sheridan ordered two of his brigades—Wagner's and Harker's—to press the retreat, but darkness slowed the pursuit. Near the foot of the ridge, both commands ran into resistance of undetermined strength. Sheridan pulled them back to the crest. By 7:00 p.m., Grant had returned to his Chattanooga headquarters, from where he sent word to General Halleck in Washington of the news of the most satisfying kind: "A complete victory. . . . I have no idea of finding Bragg here tomorrow."

Meigs echoed Grant's jubilation. "The Slave aristocracy is broken down. [Chattanooga is] the grandest stroke yet struck for our country."

Cleburne Saves the Army of Tennessee

CHAPTER NINE
NOVEMBER 27, 1863

This statue of Confederate Maj. Gen. Patrick R. Cleburne was erected in 2009, paying tribute to Cleburne's heroic defense of Ringgold Gap on November 27. Cleburne is credited with saving the Confederate army. (psir)

At midnight, Major General Sheridan received orders "to press the enemy." Rousing his men from their impromptu bivouac near Bragg's former headquarters on Missionary Ridge, Sheridan's three brigades cautiously made their way eastward, toward Chickamauga Station. Moonlight lit their way, revealing the detritus of a routed army. Wagons, caissons, discarded weapons, and equipment lay scattered before them. Of actual Confederates, however, they found few. They pressed on to the banks of Chickamauga Creek, arriving at 2:00 a.m., and halted.

In his postwar memoirs, Sheridan recalled things differently. With Grant and Thomas returned to Chattanooga, Sheridan remembered visiting Gordon Granger at Bragg's old headquarters—finding Granger already abed— and urging just such a pursuit only to be told the Army of the Cumberland "had done well enough." When Sheridan remonstrated, Granger grudgingly authorized him to go as far as the creek, and Sheridan said, "If I encountered the enemy he would order troops to my support." Reaching the creek unopposed, Sheridan next tried a bit of theater, ordering "two regiments to

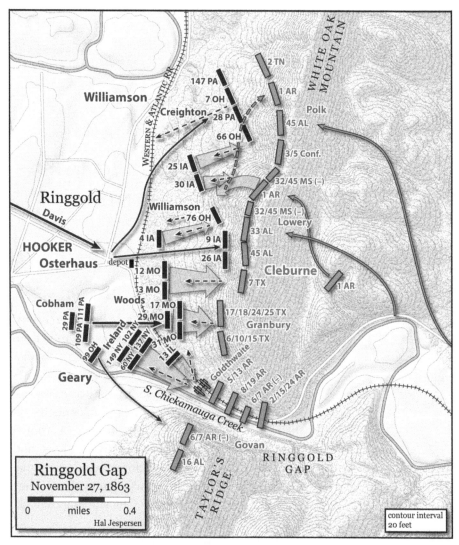

RINGGOLD GAP—The Federal pursuit of Bragg's defeated forces ground to a halt at Ringgold Gap, where Confederate divisional commander Patrick Cleburne reprised his stubborn defensive stand of November 25. After a day's fighting in which Hooker's troops made no progress, Grant halted the action. The Army of Tennessee escaped to Dalton, where it reorganized.

simulate an engagement by opening fire . . . but [the] scheme failed. General Granger afterward told me," Sheridan penned, "that he had heard the volleys" but knew them to be a ruse since they were too regular in their delivery."

At 9:00 p.m. the night before, after Bragg ascertained all the Confederates who might escape the Federal trap had reached safety, the

Confederate commander ordered all the bridges across Chickamauga Creek burned. At 2:00 a.m. on November 26, as Sheridan's men worked their way down Missionary Ridge's east face toward the creek, Bragg's army began its own movement, a retreat toward Dalton, Georgia, twenty-six miles to the southeast. At Dalton, Bragg had a secure rail connection to Atlanta and the imposing terrain of Rocky Face Ridge where the Army of Tennessee could hopefully rally and make a stand.

Union Maj. Gen. Philip H. Sheridan's aggressive pursuit of the retreating Confederates impressed Ulysses S. Grant. When Grant went east, Grant gave Sheridan command of the Army of the Potomac's Cavalry Corps. (loc)

Grant certainly intended a pursuit, but he also had to think about Knoxville. Abraham Lincoln, acutely conscious of Union General Burnside's circumstances in East Tennessee, never wasted a chance to urge Grant to Burnside's relief. Grant ordered Sherman and Thomas to follow Bragg—Sherman with his whole command, Thomas with Hooker's combined command plus Palmer's XIV Corps. Gordon Granger's IV Corps—including Sheridan's troops, who marched back into Chattanooga on November 26—would go to help Burnside. To bulk up the Knoxville expedition, Howard's XI Corps joined it, augmenting Granger's force to 20,000 men— fully sufficient, in conjunction with Burnside's strength, to deal with Longstreet.

Large quantities of Rebel supplies, painstakingly accumulated at Chickamauga Station, had to be abandoned and burned. Brigadier General Joseph Lewis's Kentucky "Orphan" Brigade drew this unpleasant duty. Men who had been on short rations for two months due to Bragg's transportation issues now watched in frustration as thousands of rations went up in smoke. At 11:00 a.m., the Kentuckians withdrew, leaving the job unfinished, as the first Union troops approached the depot. The Federals belonged to Union Brig. Gen. Jefferson C. Davis's command, who immediately set about extinguishing fires and confiscating the remaining supplies for their own use. After all, the Federals had been on even shorter rations over the past 60 days.

Bragg's intermediate destination was the railroad town of Ringgold, site of another gap through another set of ridges. His battered army first needed to move south to the hamlet of Graysville, Georgia, where the Federal Road crossed Chickamauga Creek before making its way to Ringgold. With Rossville in Union hands, however, the Confederates feared General Hooker's column following that same Federal Road could reach Graysville first.

Hooker certainly intended to get there first. Flushed with back-to-back victories at Lookout Mountain and Rossville, he now impatiently pressed ahead. Mindful of his bridging troubles on November 25 at Chattanooga Creek, Hooker this time asked for "three pontoons, with their baulks and chesses," to be sent him, but they had yet to reach him at about midday when the head of his column reached the site of Red House (also known as "Ringgold") Bridge, over the west fork of Chickamauga Creek. It took several hours before Hooker's troops had even a partial bridge, sufficient to cross infantry, in place. The pontoons did not arrive until 10:00 p.m. By then, virtually all of Bragg's army had closed on Ringgold.

Confederate Brig. Gen. Joseph H. Lewis's Kentucky "Orphan" Brigade helped destroy the stockpiled supplies at Chickamauga Depot on the morning of November 26. (loc)

On the morning of the twenty-sixth, Bragg established his headquarters at Catoosa Station, two miles south of Ringgold. At 11:30 a.m., through Confederate cavalry commander Joseph Wheeler, Bragg advised Longstreet of the disaster, and urged the latter "to fall back . . . upon Dalton, if possible." If that was "impracticable . . . you will have to fall back toward Virginia."

Toward the end of the day, Bragg laid out his plans for the twenty-seventh. The army would continue to Dalton, with a rear guard. That task fell upon Maj. Gen. Patrick Cleburne and his division, whose stalwart defense of Tunnel Hill stood as the single redeeming aspect of November

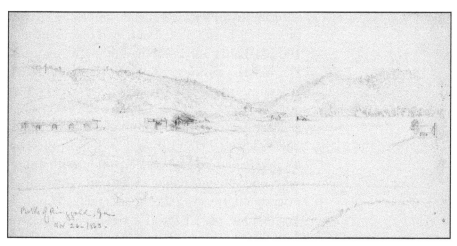

25, a day of otherwise unmitigated disaster. On the twenty-sixth, Cleburne's men had performed rear guard duties and camped just short of Ringgold. That afternoon Cleburne sent Capt. Irving A. Buck to Bragg's headquarters for additional instructions. There, an unusually emotional Bragg greeted Buck. Clasping Buck's right hand in both of his own, Bragg instructed the captain to "tell General Cleburne to hold his position at all hazards, and keep back the enemy, until the artillery and transportation of the army is secure, the salvation of which depends on him." Shocked, Buck thought Bragg "exhibited more excitement than I supposed possible for him. He had evidently not rested during the [previous] night."

Alfred Waud sketched Hooker's Federals engaging Patrick Cleburne's men at Ringgold Gap. Waud was not present for any of his western sketches—at the time of the battles for Chattanooga, he was with the Army of the Potomac on the Mine Run campaign—but the Library of Congress still describes his western sketches as wartime images. The wetern sketches were most likely completed during one of his post-war trips to the Western Theater; his work continued to be published after the war. (loc)

Cleburne's force numbered 4,157 effectives. At least one Union corps—and perhaps two— approached for a fight in the morning. Bragg's was a tall order. "'But,' said [Cleburne,] 'I always obey orders.'"

The town of Ringgold sat just west of the eponymous gap, through which flowed the Chickamauga and the tracks of the Western & Atlantic Railroad. Taylor's Ridge extended to the south; White Oak Mountain to the north. If held in force, the position offered an opportunity for a powerful defense.

On Taylor's Ridge, higher and more steeply sloped, Cleburne placed only two regiments, the 16th Alabama and combined 6th/7th Arkansas. He placed the rest of Col. Daniel Govan's Arkansas brigade in the gap, supporting two guns from Lt. Richard Goldthwaite's Alabama artillery battery; the infantry deployed in line, one regiment behind the other, for depth. The artillerymen screened their cannon with brush for concealment. Colonel Hiram Granbury's brigade of Texans held the ascending slopes of White Oak on Cleburne's right, with the 7th Texas anchoring that flank at the crest of the mountain. Brigadier Generals Lucius Polk's and Mark Lowery's two brigades were held in reserve at the southeastern foot of White Oak, just east of the gap.

Joe Hooker's Federals did not come to grips with any formed Confederate troops on November 26, but they certainly saw plenty of evidence of an army in demoralized retreat. The 13th Illinois regimental history later recorded the details: "Broken-down gun carriages, abandoned wagons, guns, ambulances, clothes, etc.," all littered the way. Additionally, "[f]or some reasons whether for good or bad, many rebels lingered in the woods. Along the way, the Union men picked up about forty or fifty prisoners." Hooker's troops camped that night a couple miles short of the gap. At 6:00 a.m. on the twenty-seventh, he turned to that "glorious soldier," General Osterhaus, to lead the pursuit again. Osterhaus's column advanced without artillery, which was still far behind due to the bridging problems.

Brushing aside a few Rebel cavalry, Osterhaus entered Ringgold around 7:00 a.m. He rode to the railroad depot, a sturdy stone structure at the foot of White Oak Mountain, a few hundred yards from the gap. From the rail platform, Osterhaus saw the tail end of a wagon train in the gap, along with a limbered artillery battery, protected only by

A Waud sketch shows the flag of Cleburne's Division. Actually, the flag, which was a white moon (usually circular, but sometimes less than full) on a blue field, was the Hardee Pattern Corps Flag. Cleburne's men retained this flag after the rest of the army was issued new Confederate battle flags in early 1864. (loc)

"a feeble line of skirmishers." Cleburne's orders to conceal Goldthwaite's cannon and for his infantry to hold their fire now paid off. Osterhaus failed to detect the Rebels arrayed on the heights or Goldthwaite's unlimbered fieldpieces, seeing only more signs of a thoroughly whipped foe.

Hooker arrived, riding through largely empty streets—most of Osterhaus's men had yet to come up. Ringgold had already been badly used in the Chickamauga campaign and was now mostly (but not entirely) deserted. Private Jacob Early of the 99th Ohio described the place as "a stinking Secesh hole, but it was [once] a rich place [with] good buildings." The day's fight visited more miseries upon the town. A local told Hooker the Rebels were in full retreat and in "disarray." Osterhaus thought he could capture the wagons, just visible in the gap, with little effort. Even though no Union cannon had arrived, due to those earlier bridging problems, Hooker ordered Osterhaus to "attack immediately." If necessary, other troops would be sent up the face of White Oak Mountain on a flanking move as they arrived.

Three Missouri regiments of Brig. Gen. Charles Woods's first brigade now made for the gap, preceded by a heavy line of skirmishers.

Woods detailed the 13th Illinois to protect his right, directing them to move past the depot and form line facing the gap, and he sent the 76th Ohio to screen the left, climbing White Oak Mountainconsiderably north of the rest of the brigade.

Almost immediately, Osterhaus ran into trouble. Granbury's Texans repulsed the Missourians, tumbling them back to the cover of the railroad embankment where, as Woods reported, "they were not again entirely rallied until after the enemy retired." The 13th Illinois faced Goldthwaite's cannon, suffering severely. The men sought cover in and around the buildings of the Isaac Jobe farm, 300 yards south of the depot and about 100 yards from the western mouth of the gap. Infantry crossfire and the deadly cannon cut the Illinoisans to pieces. When both Lt. Col. Frederick Partridge and Maj. Douglas Bushnell died in combat, command devolved to a captain. The 13th's return fire failed to silence the Rebel artillery.

With Woods stalled, Osterhaus turned to his next brigade, Iowans under Col. James Williamson's command. Osterhaus ordered Williamson's soldiers to scale White Oak Mountain, in support of the 76th Ohio still working its way up the slope. They set to it, but ended up widely dispersed. Only the 4th Iowa scaled the height close enough to remain within supporting distance of the Ohioans.

This fight would not be a repeat of Missionary Ridge. Cleburne dispatched regiments and then virtually the entire brigades of both Lowery and Polk; all scrambled up the eastern face while the Federals toiled up the other side. The 76th had ascended only with great difficulty, recalling of their climb "[t]he side of the ridge . . . covered for a great part with small, loose stones, or 'shale' which made the ascent slow and exceedingly toilsome." At the crest, they met the first of Cleburne's defenders.

Confederate brigadier Lucius Polk personally had led the first of his regiments up the ridge. The 1st Arkansas infantry, Polk reported, reached the crest to discover the enemy also "within 20 steps of the top." A furious firefight ensued, which cost the Ohioans forty percent of their 200 men, cutting down eight of the regimental color guard, and leaving the Federals pinned just short of the summit. The 4th Iowa's arrival was offset first by the combined 32nd/45th Mississippi from Lowery's command and then more Rebels from both brigades. The Rebels suffered much lighter losses, thanks to gaining the crest first; the Mississippians reported only 1 man killed and 17 wounded.

A modern view of the New York Monument in Ringgold Gap shows White Oak Mountain beyond. (hs)

As Osterhaus's assault blunted, Hooker reinforced him with Brig. Gen. John Geary's division of Easterners, though again the assaults launched in piecemeal fashion. Colonel David Ireland's New York brigade rushed directly into the gap, replacing the battered 13th Illinois. Colonel George Cobham's small three-regiment Pennsylvania brigade squared off against Granbury's men on the south end of White Oak Mountain, while Col. William Creighton, hoping to find the Rebel flank, led his mixed Ohio and

Pennsylvania brigade up the ridge even farther to the north of the 76th Ohio's position. "We marched up in line of battle," recalled Cpl. Henry Ames of the 66th Ohio, "and then made a rush for the top—for the sooner we got up the better." They did so, Ames noted, under "a shower of lead raining down upon us. . . . We had got within one hundred feet of the top when every man gave out and could go no farther."

Now, Polk and Lowery's Confederates pinned Creighton's men in a crossfire. Draws in the ridge naturally channeled Creighton's advance. By working skirmishers down these draws, men of the 2nd Tennessee and 16th Alabama soon savaged the Union flanks.

Ireland's New Yorkers fared no better, plunging into the gap. According to Lt. Edward Hopkins of the 149th New York, Ireland's brigade initially "massed behind a long railroad depot." From there, the men got a good look at Cleburne's imposing position, which "looked like a difficult place to take." Hopkins "overheard Gen. Hooker say that he could take it, but he would not sacrifice his men to do it." That must have been heartening, at least until Hooker "changed his mind when he saw the western troops on the right . . . were being driven back."

The 149th led Ireland's brigade to the right until they reached Chickamauga Creek, and then they moved directly into the gap while "exposed to a withering fire, not only from the troops along the ridge but from a battery in the gap." One shell "grazed [Hopkins's] boot" before passing though the horse of a "Capt. Green, . . . taking the captain's right leg off at the knee." The 149th broke and bolted for the cover of the Jobe barn, pinned down for the next two hours in the farm's limited shelter.

Since these Rebels were clearly not routed, broken, or dispirited, Hooker and Osterhaus abandoned any idea of a quick victory and waited

for their artillery support. When the column's guns arrived shortly after noon, Hooker ordered them to shell the ridge and gap but with little success. A while later, Grant arrived and ordered Hooker to break off the action.

Cleburne and his division performed exceedingly well, holding off the much larger Federal column by a combination of well-placed defenders, limited but well-timed counterblows, and the judicious use of reserves. His brigade commanders all handled their troops skillfully. The Federals paid a substantial price for their rashness: over 500 casualties. Cleburne, by contrast, reported "20 killed, 190 wounded, and 11 missing." Ironically, at about the time Grant ordered Hooker to break off, Cleburne prepared to do the same, after having fulfilled his mission to buy time for the rest of Bragg's army to get away safely. His division's stand earned special thanks from the Confederate Congress. For the Army of Tennessee, Ringgold Gap proved to be a small bright spark in a sea of otherwise unrelieved gloom.

The Ringgold Depot was built in 1849, serving the new Western & Atlantic Railroad, which connected Chattanooga and Atlanta. One of the more substantial buildings in the small town of Ringgold, the depot served as both cover during the fighting and as a hospital afterwards. (dp)

$\mathscr{G}rant\ \mathscr{A}scending$

CHAPTER TEN
DECEMBER 1863 TO MARCH 1864

News of Ulysses S. Grant's dramatic victory over Braxton Bragg and the Army of Tennessee reached the North at a seemingly prophetic moment since the first national day of Thanksgiving was celebrated on November 26, 1863. President Abraham Lincoln in October had issued a proclamation establishing the day in recognition of Union successes at Gettysburg and Vicksburg but at the same time when the Union circumstances in Chattanooga still looked dicey. Now, Grant's latest triumph assured the Northern public the war was indeed winnable, and Federal armies pressed onward to final victory.

Chattanooga made Grant in a way that Vicksburg's triumph had not. Within slightly more than a month of being given authority over the entire Western Theater, Grant erased the defeat of Chickamauga, saved the Army of the Cumberland, and routed Bragg. Unsurprisingly, in March 1864, Abraham Lincoln elevated Grant to Lieutenant General—a rank held by only two men before him: George Washington, promoted posthumously, and, Winfield Scott, by brevet in 1855. Grant was the first officer to actively hold that permanent rank in wartime, and he received full command of all United States armies in the

A monument to the men of Grant's home state of Illinois stands atop Orchard Knob. (cm)

This image is said to be of Confederate prisoners at the railroad depot in Chattanooga, though there are no guards in the picture and there is no date. Nevertheless, the Federals took in a rich haul of prisoners at Chattanooga: Of the 6,667 total losses, more than 4,100 were listed as missing or captured. (loc)

field. Lincoln had finally found the man who could win the war.

Conversely, Chattanooga basically ended Braxton Bragg's career. The Army of Tennessee's various tensions and turmoil came to a head after the disastrous—and seemingly inexplicable—defeat on Missionary Ridge. Bragg blamed virtually everyone but himself for the defeat, claiming that Breckinridge was drunk; that Hill, Longstreet, and Buckner had done their best to destroy the army's morale; and that even the rank and file had failed him. On November 29, Bragg detailed these complaints to Confederate Secretary of War James Seddon, calling for an investigation and, in perhaps a pro-forma offer, tendering his resignation. To Bragg's surprised anger and embarrassment, Seddon accepted that resignation quickly.

In February, Confederate President Jefferson Davis summoned Bragg to Richmond for a

new assignment, "charged with the conduct of military operations of the Confederate States." In theory, Bragg's new position mirrored Grant's. In reality, it reduced Bragg to serve as Davis's military advisor since Jefferson Davis preferred to "conduct the military operations of the Confederate States" personally. Bragg did not actively command troops again until the very end of the war. He assumed command of the defense of Wilmington, North Carolina, in October 1864, and took part with diminished authority in the coalition of ad-hoc forces opposing Sherman in the spring of 1865.

The Whitman House in Ringgold is purported to be where Grant spent the night on November 27, after the Confederates evacuated the gap. (hs)

In 1864, when Grant decided to personally oversee the conduct of the war in Virginia, he chose William T. Sherman to succeed him in command of the Department of the Mississippi. In spite of Sherman's wholly unsatisfactory performance at Chattanooga, Grant still trusted Sherman implicitly and unleashed him to carry the war to Atlanta, Savannah, and then the Carolinas.

Perhaps in an effort to justify this decision, after the war Grant's supporters—Sherman first among them—crafted a new narrative to explain what happened in November 1863. In that narrative, they reimagined Sherman's role in the battle. Far

After the victory, Grant took some time to sightsee. Like many other Union soldiers, he visited Lookout Mountain. This image is among the most famous documenting his time in the area. (loc)

from being Grant's main effort, Sherman's attack and Hooker's movement against Rossville turned into diversionary efforts, aimed at drawing Rebel force and attention to the flanks, leaving their center vulnerable. They portrayed the attack on Missionary Ridge as Grant's intended strategy all along. In his memoirs, Sherman boasted that this plan succeeded "admirably."

Joseph Hooker received the least credit for his successes at Lookout Mountain and Rossville. Grant dismissed "The Battle Above the Clouds" as mere romance, and his comments concerning Rossville primarily criticized Hooker for being too slow and exaggerating the number of prisoners taken, all suggesting Hooker simply indulged in apple-polishing to magnify his own achievements. Hooker was certainly ambitious, eager to redeem a reputation damaged by the battle of Chancellorsville, but at both the Lookout Mountain and Rossville fights, he scored real victories, greatly contributing to Grant's overall success.

Grant also had very few words of praise for George Thomas. He regarded Thomas as too slow and too cautious; Thomas's insistence in early November that the Army of the Cumberland was not ready to attack greatly colored Grant's opinions. As it turned out, Grant's stated fear that the Army of the Cumberland was too demoralized to fight well proved completely unjustified, but even in his memoirs, Grant offered only faint praise for their efforts.

Naturally, these charges sowed post-war rancor. Grant's detractors quickly pointed out the various errors and misrepresentations found in Grant's memoirs and other writings on the subject while Grant partisans leapt to their hero's defense. As a result, the various accounts describing Chattanooga tend to be weighted with partisanship toward one side or the other. Sorting fact from post-war justification can be a difficult business even today, making Chattanooga one of the more difficult challenges faced by modern historiography.

Although Grant and those in his camp might have oversold some aspects of the campaign, there can be no question that Grant made critical contributions to that victory. It fell, ultimately, on Ulysses S. Grant to make the decisions, bear the responsibility, and deal with the consequences of battle. When the battle did not go according to his plan, Grant adapted and modified that plan. A stumble in one sector met with success elsewhere, and Grant capitalized upon that success. This flexibility should not be dismissed lightly. Far too many commanders, when confronted by an unexpected reverse, responded with passivity— Braxton Bragg, for example.

Grant's victory at Chattanooga opened a critical doorway into the Confederacy's heartland, a doorway through which William T. Sherman and 100,000 fellow Federals marched the next summer. The end was in sight.

This image of Grant adorns an 1868 campaign button from Grant's first campaign for the White House. (loc)

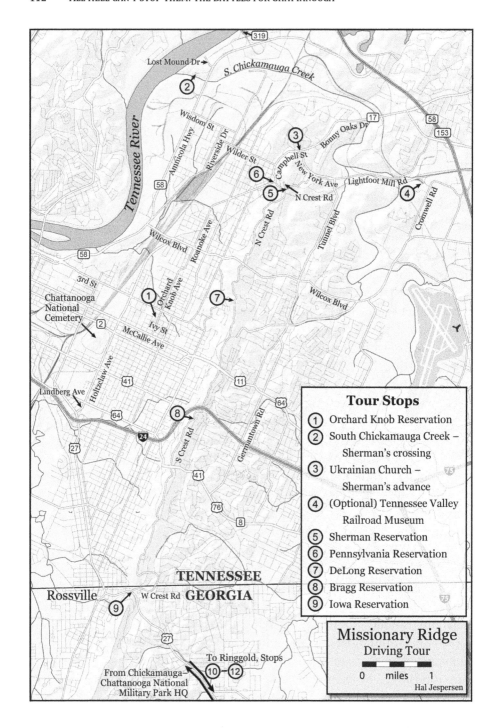

Touring the Battlefield

Many of the monuments and markers atop Missionary Ridge are really only accessible on foot. Furthermore, Crest Road, where most of these markers are located, is a residential street with very limited parking. There are two or three parking spaces at the DeLong Reservation, and a handful of parking places at the Bragg Reservation, but other than that, there is almost no place to leave your vehicle. If you have the time and ability, Missionary Ridge is best seen on foot, parking at the Bragg Reservation and then walking either north or south along the road. Bear these details in mind as you follow the driving tour below.

The best time to visit Missionary Ridge is early on a weekend morning (when traffic is at its lightest) and especially in the winter or spring when the foliage is off the trees, permitting the best views from most of the Ridge.

This tour begins at the Chickamauga-Chattanooga National Military Park Head-quarters, Fort Oglethorpe, Georgia.

GPS: N 34.94043, W 85.25994

▶ TO STOP 1

Exit the park headquarters parking lot and turn left onto La Fayette Road. North of the park this road becomes US Route 27 north. Go straight ahead and follow US 27 N through Rossville, 6.5 miles. Immediately after you pass under US Interstate 24 (I-24) turn right onto Lindberg Avenue. In one block, Lindberg Avenue ends; turn left onto Holtzclaw Avenue. In 1.6 miles, turn right onto McCallie Avenue. Proceed 6 blocks (approximately 0.3 miles) to Orchard Knob Avenue and turn left. In three blocks, at the corner of Ivy Street and Orchard Knob Avenue, you will see the Orchard Knob Reservation on your left.

The Reservation occupies the entire block between Ivy and 4th Street, Orchard Knob Avenue, and Hawthorne Street. You can circle the Reservation to locate a parking spot, if need be. Then climb Orchard Knob to the Artillery Battery and Illinois Monument in the center of the reservation.

GPS: N 35.03940, W 85.27341

Stop 1—Orchard Knob

From this point, Generals Grant, Thomas and Granger witnessed the unfolding action on November 25, 1863. Today tree growth on both Missionary Ridge and on Orchard Knob obstruct much of the modern view, but in 1863 the entire area was largely bare of timber. The assembled generals could observe most of Sherman's fighting around Tunnel Hill (to your left) and clearly see the Confederate defenses at both the foot and crest of the ridge to your east. Hooker's advance towards Rossville (on your right) was too distant to see clearly—even if the modern intrusion of Interstate 24 did not get in the way. The 3-inch ordnance rifles of Capt. Lyman Bridges's battery that you see here mark the guns that fired the signal to advance at 3:40 p.m., and the battery with which Gen. Gordon Granger spent much of his day, to General Grant's great annoyance.

→ TO STOP 2

Drive north on Orchard Knob Avenue. In 0.8 miles, Orchard Knob Avenue jogs right and becomes Roanoke Avenue. Continue onto Roanoke another 0.3 miles, and turn left onto Wilcox Avenue. In 0.7 miles, turn right onto TN Route 58, Riverside Avenue. At the next intersection, Riverside will bear off to the right; stay left and remain on Route 58, also known as Amnicola Highway.

In 2.4 miles, just after you cross South Chickamauga Creek, turn left onto Lost Mound Road. Take the very next left turn and follow the road for 0.3 miles to the Tennessee River Walk Loop.

Exit the vehicle, and follow the signs to the Riverwalk Path. In another 0.3 miles, you will reach the Tennessee River.

GPS: N 35.08919, W 85.26328

Stop 2–South Chickamauga Creek/Sherman's Crossing

Here, at the mouth of South Chickamauga Creek at the Tennessee River, Sherman's 116 assault boats first landed to establish a beachhead for the pontoon bridge to follow. The 55th Illinois and 8th Missouri Regiments led the way. They met little opposition, just a picket guard, and moved inland far enough to make room for the rest of Sherman's column. By dawn, the bridge was completed, and two of Sherman's divisions were across.

The modern Tennessee River differs greatly from the river as it was in 1863. Nickajack Dam, 45 miles downstream, has created Nickajack Lake, which stretches all the way to Chickamauga Dam, just a bit upstream. The historic river was high in November 1863, thanks to a month's worth of rain, but probably still not as wide as it normally is today.

→ TO STOP 3

Once back in your vehicle, return to TN Route 58 and turn right. In 0.7 miles, turn left onto Wisdom Street. In 0.5 miles, turn right onto Riverside Drive, and in two blocks, turn left again onto Wilder Street. In 0.7 miles Wilder will end at Campbell Street; turn left here.

Follow Campbell Street (TN Route 17) to the Ukrainian Gospel Church parking lot. Note that at the intersection of Campbell Street, Vinewood Drive, and New York Avenue, Campbell becomes Bonny Oaks Drive. The church is a short way past the intersection.

Note: The church parking lot may or may not be accessible. If parking is available, you can stop here; if not, please find a safe place to park in the immediate vicinity.

GPS: N 35.07345, W 85.23698

Stop 3—Ukrainian Church/Sherman's Advance

You are now in the valley separating Billy Goat Hill and Tunnel Hill. If you face the church's front door, Billy Goat Hill rises to your left rear and Tunnel Hill to your right rear. When Sherman cautiously advanced on the afternoon of November 24, he made for Billy Goat Hill. Only then did his skirmishers discover the valley where we are now, separating Billy Goat Hill from the main Missionary Ridge complex. Confederate skirmishers from Cleburne's division were initially placed on the lower slopes of Billy Goat Hill, behind you, until forced back across this valley to the lower slopes of Tunnel Hill. By then, fast-falling darkness precluded any larger engagement. Sherman proceeded to spend the night fortifying Billy Goat Hill.

If you are going to stop 4, see below. Otherwise, skip ahead to follow directions directly to stop 5.

➔ TO STOP 4 (Optional)

Continue east on Bonnie Oaks Drive (TN Route 17) for 1.8 miles. Take the entrance ramp on your right onto TN Route 153 South. In 1.1 miles, exit TN 153 South at Exit 3, onto Jersey Pike. In 0.1 miles, turn right onto Cromwell Road. In 0.5 miles, turn right into the parking lot of the Tennessee Valley Railroad Museum.

GPS: N 35.06683, W 85.20619

Stop 4 – Tennessee Valley Railroad Museum

Although the Tennessee Valley Railroad Museum doesn't include a great deal of Civil-War specific interpretation, it does offer the interested visitor a chance to see Missionary Ridge from a unique perspective: via the historic railroad tunnel that gives Tunnel Hill its name. Most days (check the website for scheduling: *http://www.tvrail.com/*) the museum offers train rides through Missionary Ridge. The trip lasts 55 minutes, costs (as of this writing) $17 per adult, and takes you through the tunnel twice, once headed westbound and again on the return trip. Please note that the museum is not the site of wartime Chickamauga Station, which was farther south, and is now covered by the Chattanooga Airport.

→ TO STOP 5 from Stop 4

Exit the railroad museum and turn left onto Cromwell Road. In 0.7 miles, turn left onto Jersey Pike, cross under TN Route 153, and turn left onto the northbound ramp for TN Route 153. In 0.5 miles, take the next exit, Exit 4 onto Bonny Oaks Road (TN Route 317), turning left at the bottom of the ramp.

In 0.4 miles, turn left onto Lightfoot Mill Road. You will follow Lightfoot Mill Road for 2.5 miles. Just after you pass Durand Avenue (but staying on Lightfoot Mill Road), you will see the Sherman Reservation on your right, and a limited parking area on your left.

→ TO STOP 5 directly from Stop 3

Head west on Bonny Oaks (TN Route 317) to the intersection of New York Avenue.

Turn left on New York Avenue and travel 0.4 miles. Turn right onto New Jersey Avenue. In another 0.2 miles, turn left onto Lightfoot Mill Road. In 0.3 miles, just after you pass Durand Avenue (but staying on Lightfoot Mill Road), you will see the Sherman Reservation on your right, and a limited parking area on your left.

GPS: N 35.06575, W 85.24050

Stop 5 – The Sherman Reservation

The Sherman Reservation has been closed to vehicle traffic many years because is remote from the main park and not easily patrolled by law enforcement. While I have never  had a problem while visiting the Sherman Reservation, be forewarned that it has been a problem area in the past. That said, it is the largest piece of the Missionary Ridge battlefield preserved by the Park Service, and well worth visiting.

You will have to walk up the small road (N. Crest Road) or follow the foot trail up the hill, to reach the crest of Tunnel Hill. You will pass the foot trail down to the 73rd Pennsylvania Reservation, at the western foot of Missionary Ridge; remember the trail, as you will follow it later.

If you walk up the road, note the monuments on the side of the slope above you, especially the 93rd Illinois Infantry. Colonel Holden Putnam, mounted and clasping the colors under his arm, was killed here as he led his regiment up the hill.

At the top of the hill, you will see the cannon of a Confederate battery, and, to the north, an Iowa Monument. The guns represent Cleburne's position, and the Iowa Monument shows where Colonel Jones's Ohioans and Brig. Gen. John M. Corse's mixed brigade reached the abandoned Confederate works.

→ TO STOP 6

Tour stop 6 is best accessed on foot, as there is no safe parking at the 73rd Pennsylvania

Reservation. Take the trail leading from the Sherman Reservation. It is an easy walk, although you will be climbing the hill on the return.

GPS: N 35.06703, W 85.24363

The Pennsylvania Reservation marks the position of Buschbeck's brigade.

➤ TO STOP 7

Return to your car, and head west on Lightfoot Mill Road. In 200 feet, turn left onto N. Crest Road. Travel 2.0 miles south on N. Crest Road, until you reach the DeLong Reservation. There are several parking spots here.

As you drive the length of Crest Road, you will see a large number of monuments, markers, and tablets. Although viewable from the road, many of these features are actually on private property, so please be careful and respectful.

GPS: N 35.04292, W 85.25364

Stop 7—DeLong Reservation

The DeLong reservation marks the spot where Col. Ferdinand Van Derveer's brigade of Baird's division, Union XIV Corps, ascended Missionary Ridge. The large monument you see ahead of you honors the 2nd Minnesota Infantry, of Van Derveer's brigade. The defenders here were Water's battery of Alabama artillery, who lost almost all their cannon, and Deas's Alabama infantry brigade.

➤ TO STOP 8

Proceed south on Crest Road, for another 1.9 miles until you reach the Bragg Reservation. Turn left into the parking lot.

Note: Along the way you will pass first the Turchin Reservation and then the Ohio Reservation, neither of which has much room for parking. If you do find parking nearby, feel free to stop to visit both locations. Also, take note of the many markers, tablets and cannon denoting unit positions as you head south on Crest Road.

GPS: N 35.01888, W 85.26376

Stop 8 – Bragg Reservation

The Bragg Reservation is so named because this is where General Bragg located his headquarters, above the Moore house (down the ridge to the west) and fully visible to the Union commanders assembled on Orchard Knob. Take note of the large Illinois monument near the parking lot, and the various tablets here.

Of special note is the 24th Wisconsin marker, just a short walk along Crest Drive south of the Bragg Reservation. Here, Lt. Arthur McArthur (father of World War Two and Korean War General Douglas McArthur) was awarded the Congressional Medal of Honor for his gallant service on November 25, 1863. After the 24th's color bearer fell, eighteen-year-old Adjutant McArthur (in the words of the citation) "seized the colors of his regiment at a critical moment and planted them on the captured works on the crest of Missionary Ridge."

⟶ **TO STOP 9**

Return to Crest Road, turn left. Follow S. Crest Road for 3.6 miles; watch carefully, as the road curves and winds quite a bit. When you reach the stop light at the intersection of US Route 27 (Chickamauga Avenue) and S. Crest Road, turn right onto US Route 27. In 0.7 miles, you will see the Iowa Monument on your right, at the intersection of US Route 27 and W. Crest Road. US Route 27 curves to the left here, but before you pass W. Crest Road, there will be several parking spots along the east side before and in front of the monument.

GPS: N 34.98374, W 85.27946

Stop 9—Iowa Reservation at Rossville Gap

The gap here was defended by the 42nd and 43rd Georgia Infantry, supported by Anderson's battery of Georgia artillery. The Georgians were deployed on the rise directly east of (behind) the Iowa Monument. The nearest other Confederates were the rest of Maj. Gen. A. P. Stewart's division, more than a mile north. The actual gap in Missionary Ridge curves off to the southeast; you drove through the gap as you turned onto Route 27 from S. Crest Road.

The Federals approached from the west, led by the 27th Missouri Infantry. Colonel Williamson's Iowa brigade, of Osterhaus's division (the units to which this monument is dedicated) scaled the ridge to your

south and outflanked the Georgians, who retreated eastward to protect a Confederate wagon train. Once the Gap was secured, then General Hooker deployed his three divisions astride the ridge to your north, facing north, and ordered them to advance. They successfully unraveled Bragg's southern flank as the Rebel center was collapsing two miles to the north, near Bragg's headquarters.

Several tablets scattered around the immediate area describe the action here. Unfortunately nothing remains of General Hooker's approach route or the Confederate defenses that once stretched across Chattanooga Valley towards Lookout Mountain.

This completes the tour of Missionary Ridge. Stops 10 and 11 are in Ringgold, approximately 12 miles to the southeast.

➤ TO STOP 10

From US Route 27 at the Iowa Reservation, turn right onto W. Crest Road. Travel 0.3 miles to S. Crest Road and turn right. (Note: this is a very hard right; do not turn onto John Ross Road or Missionaire Avenue.) At the intersection of S. Crest Road and US Route 27, turn left onto US Route 27

Travel 1.7 miles to GA Route 2, Battlefield Parkway, and turn left at that stoplight. Stay on GA Route 2 for 7.7 miles, until you reach US Route 41. Turn right and travel 1.5 miles on US Route 41. At Depot Street, turn left and park in front of the Railroad Depot Building.

GPS: N 34.91523, W 85.10787

Stop 10—Ringgold Depot

(hs)

Built in 1849, this building is now owned by the City of Ringgold. It once served the Western & Atlantic Railroad and witnessed a number of important Civil War events. The great railroad chase culminated here in the spring of 1862. Ringgold was the scene of fighting in September 1863, just before the battle of Chickamauga, and became the focal point of a larger action on November 27, 1863.

Confederate Maj. Gen. Patrick Cleburne positioned his division on the ridges and within the gap east of the depot (behind it as you face the front of the building). His command was Braxton Bragg's rear guard, ordered to hold the gap long enough for the rest of Bragg's battered Army of Tennessee to make its way to Dalton, Georgia, 15 miles to the southeast. There, behind the imposing edifice of Rocky Face Ridge, Bragg's army could rest and recuperate.

The fighting here at Ringgold began when Union General Joe Hooker sent troops into the gap. They were repulsed with loss, which induced Hooker to attempt to gain the ridge crests on both sides of the gap—efforts that were all successfully rebuffed. Colonel David Ireland's New York brigade was at one point massed where you are now standing, behind what one of them described as "a long railroad depot," until they moved into action.

⟶ TO STOP 11

From the depot, turn around and head south on Depot Street. Cross US Route 41 (Nashville Street) and continue on Depot for another 0.5 miles. On your left, in front of a fenced area and some storage buildings, you will see a monument that honors the participation of New York regiments in the fight here at Ringgold. If you proceed a little farther, you will come to a small parking area along the bank of South Chickamauga Creek.

GPS: N 34.90858, W 85.10441

Stop 11–New York Monument

You have moved down into the mouth of Ringgold Gap. The tracks on your left follow the path of the Western & Atlantic. The Gap has been widened considerably in order to make room for Interstate 75, which you can observe running on the far side of the creek.

This spot marks the high point in the advance of the 13th Illinois Infantry, who suffered severely here, and also of the 149th New York, Ireland's brigade, which replaced the 13th. Two Confederate cannon, placed in the gap, were able to concentrate a heavy fire on the Federals who reached this ground. Some of the surviving Federals used the raised railroad bed for cover, until they eventually withdrew.

➡ TO STOP 12

Drive north on Depot Street for 0.5 miles, until you reach US Route 41 (Nashville Street). Turn right and proceed approximately 0.5 miles until you see a small turnout and parking area on the right. A statue of Confederate General Patrick Cleburne stands here.

GPS: N 34.90971, W 85.10274

Stop 12—Ringgold Atlanta Campaign Pavilion

(hs)

This wayside—officially, the Ringgold Atlanta Campaign Pavilion—was created by the Works Progress Administration in the 1930s, the first of five such pavilions constructed in order to commemorate the Atlanta Campaign. (The others are all on Route 41, at Dalton, Resaca, Cassville, and Dallas, Georgia.) The Cleburne Statue was erected, in 2009, by the Cleburne Society to commemorate Cleburne's determined defensive stand here at Ringgold.

(psjr)

This ends our tour of Missionary Ridge and Ringgold.

Shrouded in fog, the Ohio Monument crowns Missionary Ridge north of the Bragg Reservation.
(hs)

The drummer boy on the Ohio Monument. (hs)

The Best-Planned Battle!

APPENDIX A

Almost every Civil War battle has generated controversy, usually having to do with credit or blame. The battles for Chattanooga, involving as they did multiple Union armies sent from various theaters to save the battered Army of the Cumberland in the wake of Chickamauga, certainly produced their share. The Army of the Cumberland men resented the fact that General Rosecrans had been replaced, that General Grant had arrived to take charge, that Grant had believed them to be demoralized and incapable of offensive action, and that Sherman's men had been regarded as the more reliable force in an engagement. Over time those factors, coupled with some increasingly grandiose claims from Grant and his supporters, produced considerable disagreement about what had occurred on November 25, 1863. Conflicting views would be aired in the post-war literature for decades to come.

Among the most enduring controversies to emerge from the fighting on November 25 regarded the charge of the Army of the Cumberland up Missionary Ridge. Was it planned or spontaneous? Who ordered it? Opinions, as might be predicted, varied considerably.

The charge was, of course, wildly successful. Not surprisingly, when the time came to take credit (as opposed to assigning blame) plenty of people lined up to do so, people ranging from the overall commander on down. But as described in chapter seven, in the moment of execution, many of those involved had different interpretations of what was expected.

That controversy began at the very top, among the senior commanders gathered on Orchard Knob: Grant, Thomas, and Granger. All three men were together through the afternoon, observing the battle as it unfolded. However, when the time came to send the Army of the Cumberland's four divisions against the Confederate center on Missionary Ridge, one key query proves a sticking point: Did Grant merely intend to make a demonstration against the Rebel works at the foot of the ridge, precluding a frontal assault to the crest;

This house has been variously identified as Rosecrans's, Thomas's, and Sherman's headquarters. It was the Department of the Cumberland's headquarters in Chattanooga. (loc)

or did he always intend to storm the heights? Was the charge spontaneous invention or merely dutiful anticipation of Grant's next order?

Dated December 23, a month after the fight, Grant's report claimed the latter. Grant wrote that he ordered the Army of the Cumberland "to carry the rifle pits at the foot of Missionary Ridge, and when carried to reform [its] lines on the rifle pits with a view to carrying the top of the ridge." However, he added, "they commenced the ascent . . . from right to left almost simultaneously, following closely the retreating enemy, without further orders."

Thomas's and Granger's versions differed, both with Grant and with each other. General Thomas reported that the orders were to "move . . . against the enemy's rifle pits on the slope and at the foot of Missionary Ridge. . . . [and that] the enemy, seized with panic, abandoned the works at the foot of the hill . . . closely followed by our troops, who apparently inspired by the impulse of victory, carried the hill simultaneously at six different points." While the two descriptions were not very different, Thomas's version—dated December 1, a mere six days after the event—identified only the Rebel works at the foot and half-way up the ridge as the assault's objectives. "The impulse of victory" rather than any orders led his men to storm the crest. And Gordon Granger's report, dated February 11, 1864, contradicted Grant much more explicitly.

Granger stated flatly that he "was ordered to make a demonstration upon the works . . . at the base of Missionary Ridge" and only at the base. Once those were taken, Granger noted, "my orders had now been fully and successfully carried out." As for going farther, "they started without orders along the whole line . . . animated with one spirit and with heroic courage."

The timing of these three reports is important. Thomas's report pre-dates Grant's, so he certainly could not have seen Grant's final draft before submitting his own. Granger's was turned in six weeks *after* Grant's, and it is possible that Granger had already seen Grant's report before finishing his own. Granger had also been repeatedly rebuked by Grant: first for spending too much time fooling around with an artillery battery on Orchard Knob and rebuked again when he raised Grant's ire by sending a sarcastic telegram on Christmas Day from Knoxville, where Granger and Burnside enjoyed a holiday feast in the supposedly short-rationed town.

As can be seen in chapter seven, the men tasked with executing Grant's order were equally unclear about the ultimate objective. Three of the four division commanders believed they were to stop at the base; only Baird received word that storming the crest would follow next. For the rest, the best that can be said is that once at the foot, they were to await further orders.

Less formally, several observers on Orchard Knob left contemporary evidence as well, observers including Montgomery Meigs and Charles H. Dana. Both were there under official auspices, Meigs in his role as quartermaster general and Dana as Stanton's personal representative. Meigs left a personal journal documenting his time in Chattanooga. In his entry for November 25, Meigs recorded Grant as saying that the ascent "was contrary to orders, it was not [Grant's] plan—he meant to form the lines and then prepare and launch columns of assault; but, as the men, carried away by their enthusiasm had gone so far, he would not order them back." This comment squared

Headquarters wagons, such as this one for the Army of the Cumberland, were mobile offices, designed to allow the staff to conduct business in the field. The Army of the Cumberland also established a more permanent headquarters in Chattanooga, which functioned from September 1863 until after the end of the Atlanta Campaign in October 1864. (loc)

reasonably well with Grant's published report, and it provides some contemporary corroboration of Grant's intentions, or at least as he related them to Meigs.

Dana reported something considerably different. At 10:00 a.m. the next morning, Dana described the charge this way:

> *The storming of the ridge by our troops was one of the greatest miracles in military history. . . . Neither Grant nor Thomas intended it. Their orders were to carry the rifle pits along the base of the ridge . . . but when this was accomplished the unaccountable spirit of the troops bore them bodily up those impractical steeps. . . . The order to storm appears to have been given simultaneously by Generals Sheridan and Wood, because the men were not held back, dangerous as the attempt appeared to military prudence. Besides, the generals had caught the inspiration of the men, and were ready themselves to undertake impossibilities.*

Clearly, Dana's version is much more in keeping

with Granger's version of what happened, and—to a certain extent—Thomas's report.

Taken together, these accounts suggest that while Grant could well have intended to send Thomas's men up the ridge if the initial attack were successful, he failed to fully convey at the outset that intent to the men involved. Quite likely, his thinking was outpaced by events. And if the discussion had ended there, the whole question of what was ordered and what was not would have remained a minor footnote in the history of the battle of Missionary Ridge.

After the war, however, Grant was the man who won that war. He ascended to the presidency, in 1868, largely due to that fame. His two terms in that office were marked with controversy and corruption. His supporters worked assiduously to build him up; his detractors labored just as hard to tarnish anything he touched. His military reputation proved fair game, and Chattanooga proved a fertile subject for both camps.

William T. Sherman's memoirs, which first appeared in 1875, typify the efforts to elevate Grant—and not coincidentally, himself. Sherman did not perform well in November 1863 and had a vested interest in protecting his own reputation. After all, he became General of the Army after Grant moved into the White House. Twelve years on, Sherman argued that Chattanooga "was a magnificent battle in its conception, in its execution and in its glorious results . . . so completely successful, that nothing is left for cavil or fault-finding." From the very start "the object of General Hooker's and my attacks on the extreme flanks of Bragg's position was . . . to detach from his center . . . so that Thomas's army could break through. . . . The whole plan succeeded admirably."

In an article appearing in 1885, Adam Badeau, who served on Grant's staff and was later a close friend, confidante and biographer of the general, boldly asserted "that this battle was fought as nearly according to the plan laid down in advance as any recorded in the schools." While Grant didn't go quite so far in his own memoirs, he came close: "My recollection is that my first orders for the battle of Chattanooga were as fought. Sherman was to get on Missionary Ridge, as he did; Hooker to cross the North end of Lookout Mountain, as he did, sweep across Chattanooga Valley and get across the south end of the ridge near Rossville. When Hooker secured that position the Army of the Cumberland was to assault the center."

Of course, plenty of people knew otherwise. George Thomas had died in 1870 and Granger in 1876, but others were willing to take up the gauntlet. In one such article, Gen. William F. Smith pointed out that Sherman *never* "got on" Missionary Ridge; that Hooker's move against Rossville was more of an afterthought, decided only after Bragg evacuated Lookout Mountain; and that Thomas's assault on the center was a demonstration designed to take pressure off Sherman, not the other way around. Far from being carefully planned, the fighting that has come to be known collectively as "the Battle of Chattanooga" was for Grant largely a series of happy accidents produced by officers and troops he expressed no faith in, while his star performers— Sherman and the Army of the Tennessee—failed to make any headway.

The controversy continues to the present day. Since the historic record is contradictory, there is room for varied interpretation. Grant has come under a new wave of criticism by authors such as Benson Bobrick who critiques Grant harshly in his *Master of War, The Life of General George H. Thomas* (2010), and even more convincingly, Joseph A. Rose who puts Grant under intense scrutiny in his carefully researched *Grant Under Fire: An Expose of Generalship & Character in the American Civil War* (2015). Rose is especially meticulous in uncovering Grant's various versions of what occurred at Chattanooga.

Still, historian and Grant biographer Brooks Simpson, in a well-written and closely argued examination of the controversy over the Missionary Ridge assault, argues that "it must be kept in mind that an assault up Missionary Ridge . . . was always part of the discussion, not a spur-of-the-moment decision undertaken in haste," and as such, Grant's intent was clear. Less convincingly, Simpson blames any confusion on the Army of the Cumberland's "inability to transmit orders so as to admit of no misunderstanding." For this reasoning, Simpson relied primarily on Meigs's observations; in doing so, however, he bypassed Dana's contrary assertion as wired to Edwin Stanton on November 26. Both Meigs and Dana were present on Orchard Knob, neither were part of the Army of the Cumberland, and yet each of them walked away with contradictory views of what happened. Given those two accounts, it seems the root cause of any confusion might lie with Grant himself. To be fair, Simpson certainly did not buy into the Grant-Sherman-Badeau argument of a meticulously crafted and well-planned battle. In his biography of the general, the historian noted that "Grant no doubt contemplated an assault by Thomas in support of Sherman; [but] that he planned what happened strains credulity."

The Tower at Bleak House, Longstreet's Headquarters during the siege of Knoxville. Confederate sharpshooters operated from here. (dp)

End-Game in East Tennessee
APPENDIX B

One of the pressing reasons Grant quickly ended his pursuit of the Confederate Army of Tennessee after the action at Ringgold was the matter of relieving Knoxville. Once the telegraph wires between Knoxville and the rest of the Union were cut on November 18, neither Grant nor the War Department in Washington had more than the sketchiest communications with Burnside. That commander's last message had been optimistic, perhaps because Grant had previously told Burnside relief would come quickly. On November 15, for example, Grant informed Burnside that he should need to hold out only "seven more days."

Then came delay after delay. Grant was unable to move on November 21, despite informing Washington that he was ready to advance—a washed out pontoon bridge at Brown's Ferry derailed that move, and ultimately stranded Gen. Peter Osterhaus's division on the wrong side of the Tennessee River. Slow progress on the twenty-second precluded any offensive action that day as well. November 23 saw the capture of Orchard Knob, but Sherman's move across the Tennessee on November 24 ended disappointingly. Only Hooker's unlooked-for triumph on Lookout Mountain brightened November 24.

November 25 at last produced the signal victory Grant was hoping for, driving Bragg off Missionary Ridge, severing all rail connection between Bragg and Longstreet, and forcing Bragg to fall back into North Georgia. But even then, two days had to be devoted to pursuing Bragg's beaten force, ensuring that the Confederates did not regroup short of Dalton, and thus pose some sort of renewed threat to Chattanooga as Grant at long last turned his attention directly to Ambrose Burnside's beleaguered command forted-up in Knoxville.

Throughout the eighteen-day siege, Burnside remained optimistic, even arguing that his retreat into the Knoxville defenses (instead of trying to maintain a forward defense) helped Grant by drawing Longstreet's men farther away from Bragg. Knoxville's defensive works were very strong, expertly laid out by

James Longstreet longed for independent command. He saw East Tennessee as the opportunity he'd hoped for. (loc)

Union Capt. Orlando M. Poe, and very nearly complete by the time the Federal forces reached the city. Burnside was confident they could not be taken.

Unknown to the Federals, Bragg further aided Grant on November 22 when he dispatched yet more men to reinforce Longstreet. Bragg sent two divisions, a total of perhaps 8,000 troops, hoping that with these reinforcements, Longstreet could gain a quick knock-out blow at Knoxville and then hurry back south with his whole force to help defeat Grant. That hope was dashed the very next day, when Sherman's and Hooker's movements threatened Bragg's flanks. The Confederate commander immediately counter-manded the reinforcement order, halting Cleburne's division in its tracks, which allowed Hardee to rush them to Tunnel Hill in the nick of time. For two of the three brigades in Bushrod Johnson's division, however, the counter-order came too late.

Johnson reported that the first of his men departed Chickamauga Station on the evening of November 22, arriving at Loudoun on the twenty-fourth, and reached Longstreet on the twenty-seventh. The remainder of his command closed up on the twenty-eighth. Johnson reported his effective strength at 2,625; or, counting officers, about 3,000 troops present for duty. The two brigades included Brig. Gen. Archibald Gracie's Alabamans and Johnson's own old brigade, now led by Col. John S. Fulton, of four Tennessee regiments. "This force," appended Johnson, "was badly shod and poorly clad." They had not found easy living in the Confederate lines encircling Chattanooga. Longstreet's precarious supply situation would only impose on them additional hardships.

On the evening of November 25, Bragg's chief engineer, Brig. Gen. Danville Leadbetter, arrived at Longstreet's headquarters to reiterate the need for an immediate attack. But how? After surveying the situation over the next two days, Leadbetter remained adamant "that something should be done quickly." As a result, newly reinforced and under

pressure from Bragg, early on November 29, James
Longstreet launched what would prove to be his only
direct test of Burnside's defensive lines: a frontal
attack on the Union strongpoint of Fort Sanders,
newly named for Burnside's cavalry commander,
Brig. Gen. William P. Sanders. (On November 18,
Sanders had fallen, mortally wounded, in a rear-
guard action, and the earthen strongpoint became
his memorial.) That November 29 attack, due
to a mix of Confederate bungling and the innate
strength of the Union position, was an utter failure.
The Confederates suffered 813 casualties: 129
killed, 458 wounded, and 226 prisoners—including
a number of men who found they could not retreat
under fire and chose to surrender instead. Federal
losses amounted to 5 killed and 8 wounded. The
disaster created additional rifts between Longstreet
and some of his subordinates and convinced the
Rebels that there was no chance of taking Knoxville
by direct assault.

That same day Longstreet received updated
news from President Davis concerning Bragg
at Chattanooga. Longstreet already knew that
Grant's men were stirring on November 23; now he
discovered that Bragg had "retired before superior
numbers," and that Davis instructed Longstreet to
"cooperate" with the Army of Tennessee. Initially
Longstreet began preparations to fall back toward
Georgia, but following that instruction soon
proved impossible. Other dispatches, received that
afternoon, placed strong Union forces at Cleveland,
Tennessee. There was no chance that Longstreet's
small command could take on the 80,000 Federals
now standing between him and Bragg's army.

After the fall of Missionary Ridge, Grant's
thoughts had turned almost immediately to
relieving Knoxville. At 7:30 p.m. on November
25, he informed General Halleck that he would
immediately "move a force . . . on to the Rail
Road between Cleveland and Dalton and send
a column of twenty thousand men up the south
side of the Tennessee" toward Knoxville. Grant
ordered Sherman to send Oliver O. Howard's XI

This view of Fort Sanders in Knoxville shows a bit of the parapet, the ditch, and the tree stumps beyond. Union troops wove telegraph wire between those stops as an additional obstacle to any approaching attackers. (loc)

Corps to Cleveland with orders to sever the rail line, while Gordon Granger was tasked with marching to Knoxville. By the twenty-seventh, Howard was in place, and Granger was ready to begin moving north.

According to the 36th Illinois Infantry's regimental history, the column left Chattanooga just after midday on November 28, "after a heavy rain, which made the mud ankle deep." By the thirtieth, it reached the Hiawassee River and was ferried over to the north bank. Since the Federals controlled the rivers, Granger could rely on steamboats for resupply, a decided advantage over the Confederates. The march was cold, but the local civilians turned out to greet the men in blue, whom most regarded as liberators. By December 4, the Federals were within 15 miles of Knoxville.

Longstreet was gone, despite expecting reinforcements of his own. In response to the crisis, Longstreet asked that Maj. Gen. Robert Ransom's division from Southwest Virginia move to join him in subduing Burnside. Ransom's force was sizeable—6,300 troops, half cavalry and half infantry and artillery—but before they could even hope to arrive, Longstreet captured a courier (a plant by Grant, as it turned out, intended to force Longstreet's retreat) from Grant to Burnside, detailing a series of Union movements. According to the missive, three columns were set to converge on Longstreet's small army: "one by the south side [of the Tennessee] under General Sherman; one by Dechard [Tennessee] under General [Washington] Elliott, and one by Cumberland Gap, under General [John G.] Foster." Faced with multiple threats, Longstreet chose to move north toward Virginia, bypassing Knoxville's northern defenses on December 2.

In his memoirs, Sherman noted that Grant wanted him to take personal charge of the main relief column because Grant thought that Granger, "instead of moving with great rapidity as ordered, seemed to move 'slowly, and with reluctance.'" Grant's fretfulness was triggered by information from Burnside suggesting that the latter officer only had food enough to hold out until December 3, leaving a mere six days to cover the 110 miles from Chattanooga to Knoxville, trudging through muddied roads and across unbridged rivers.

Granger was certainly unhappy with the assignment, regarding East Tennessee as a backwater, but Sherman was no more enthusiastic about the mission. "Recollect that East Tennessee is my horror," he informed Grant, adding "that any military man should send a force into East Tennessee puzzles me." Sherman was referring to his own time in command of the Department of the Ohio, back in the fall of 1861, when the Lincoln administration was hounding him about East Tennessee. Puzzled or not, Sherman was now headed to Knoxville.

On December 6, Sherman and Granger rode into Knoxville. To his surprise, Sherman rode past a corral containing a "fine lot of cattle, which did not look much like starvation." After an inspection of the Union lines, including Fort Sanders, the generals "sat down to a good dinner, embracing roast turkey." Burnside explained that Longstreet's men had never been able to completely isolate the Federals, and supplies continued to reach him via the south side of the Tennessee River, which explained the apparent largesse; the fact that Longstreet had been gone for four days was also a boon, allowing yet more foodstuffs to pour in. It was a recent bounty, however: Burnside's men had been on half-rations just a few days previous, and his livestock, like Thomas's, were suffering from want of forage.

After conferring, Sherman left Granger with two divisions to support Burnside and help pursue Longstreet, who was headed to Rogersville, 65 miles northeast of Knoxville. Again Granger expressed anger and annoyance at being exiled, "complaining bitterly of what he thought was hard treatment. . . ." Granger's complaints accomplished nothing except to make up Sherman's mind to replace Granger at the next opportunity. Granger's soldiers were equally unhappy, facing a winter campaign amid great hardships. On December 7, Col. Francis T. Sherman of the 88th Illinois noted the "men on short rations, very tired and shoes worn out."

Longstreet's Confederates slogged into Rogersville on December 9, after a grueling march. All along the way, the Rebel column shed men, some too sick to keep up, others who lacked the will to fight on—either because they were Unionists at heart or simply disheartened. According to historian Earl Hess, in his study of the East Tennessee campaign, a quarter of the Rebel prisoners taken at Knoxville lacked shoes. They looked "like heathens, so ragged & dirty & even barefooted." The rest went into camp around Rogersville and sent out forage parties. Longstreet believed he could remain in East Tennessee only if the rail line from Virginia could be placed into operation; currently, it ran only as far as the state line. On December 10, President Davis ordered Longstreet to assume command of all the Rebel forces then in East Tennessee, including those forces on loan from Maj. Gen. Samuel Jones's Department of Southwest Virginia.

Meanwhile, Burnside did not hasten to pursue the Confederate force. Leaving Granger's men to hold Knoxville, he pushed elements of the IX Corps in Longstreet's direction. However, the nearest they came to Longstreet's Rogersville camps was Bean's

Station, some 20 miles to the southwest. No longer in danger of encirclement, Longstreet decided on a counterattack. On the afternoon of December 14, Longstreet assaulted the 4,000 Federals at Bean's Station, employing Johnson's (formerly Buckner's), McLaws's, and elements of Hood's (Jenkins's) divisions, plus cavalry—perhaps 6,000 to 7,000 men in all. The fight lasted into the next day, with results largely in Longstreet's favor, although the Federals managed to avoid entrapment and fell back toward Knoxville.

Bean's Station marked the end of the campaign. By the next spring, East Tennessee—once considered so vital—would be largely denuded of troops, though Knoxville remained firmly in Union hands for the rest of the war. Longstreet and his men would return to the welcome embrace of Robert E. Lee and the Army of Northern Virginia. Wheeler's Confederate Cavalry Corps, much ravaged by their time in the region, returned to the Army of Tennessee, now led by Joseph E. Johnston. Burnside and the IX Corps would also travel east, brought to Virginia to reinforce George G. Meade's Army of the Potomac.

One of the casualties of Longstreet's East Tennessee campaign was division commander Maj. Gen. Lafayette McLaws. Longstreet blamed the failure of the campaign, in part, on McLaws, and their falling out ended in a court martial. McLaws was returned to service, though, and served during the Carolinas campaign. (nps)

Gordon Granger was granted his wish to escape East Tennessee, though likely he was not happy with the resultant transfer. On December 25, Granger further eroded his already-tenuous position with Grant and Sherman by sending a sarcastic telegram to Grant in Nashville. Granger, who was probably intoxicated at the time, wired that "we are in Knoxville and will hold it until hell freezes over." After reading the missive, Grant deemed Granger to be "a trifler unworthy of high command or great responsibilities." As a result, when the IV Corps marched back to Chattanooga that spring to join General Sherman's army readying for the Atlanta campaign, Oliver O. Howard—not Gordon Granger—led the corps. Granger found himself without a command until, later that year, he was assigned to the District of West Florida and South Alabama in the Department of the Gulf, where he participated in Union operations against Mobile.

A Monumental Struggle

APPENDIX C
BY WILLIAM LEE WHITE

On the late autumn afternoon of November 25, 1863, a massive wave of Union soldiers surged toward the awaiting and awestruck Confederate line just east of Chattanooga in what would be the defining moment of the struggle for the city. On the left of the assault, Union Brig. Gen. Absalom Baird's brigades advanced toward Carroll House Knoll, a prominent projecting spur of Missionary Ridge. From the knoll, Confederate cannon unleashed a fire that Baird subsequently characterized as "severe; the atmosphere seemed filled with the messengers of death and shells burst in every direction." Through this shell storm, his three brigades plunged. Two brigades captured the line of Confederate rifle pits in front of and to the north of the knoll.

Baird's third brigade, Brig. Gen. John Turchin's, struggled on through difficult ground on the divisional right, lagging behind the forward edge of the rest of the command. Finally, Turchin's men surged forward with great momentum to make up for their lost time. Upon hitting the picket line, they didn't seem to stop but pushed up the slopes of Missionary Ridge. In doing so, they joined Brig. Gen. Tom Wood's division to Turchin's right, which a short time before had started its own assault up the steeply sloped ridge. Seeing Turchin, the rest of Baird's division began a similar ascent. Suddenly the whole Union force was moving, 20,000 strong.

Turchin's surge carried his command up the ridge so quickly that his was the first in the division to plant its colors at the crest. The Confederates in the division's front broke into full retreat at the sight of this onslaught. Once up, Turchin now pushed his regiments to the right and left to clear the Confederate line on either flank, making way for the rest of Baird's men and Wood's command. In doing so, Turchin's men became intermingled

The 2nd Minnesota Monument was the subject of much debate between General John Turchin and Park Historian Henry V. Boynton after the war. (hs)

Many veterans returned to visit the battlefields of Chickamauga and Chattanooga. Here, the surviving members of Knap's Pennsylvania Battery pose with the monument to their command on the west side of Orchard Knob. (pacc)

with those of Col. Ferdinand Van Deveer's brigade (also of Baird's division), which was then making its way up the front and north faces of Carroll's knoll. The rapidly deteriorating situation quickly convinced any lingering Confederates in the area to begin making their escape.

Turchin's and Van Deveer's comingled commands swept over the last of those Rebels who remained, capturing cannon, men, and flags as twilight settled over the field. That hour would become one of the most celebrated in the Army of the Cumberland's long history, an instant of redemption from defeat at Chickamauga and the moment the Federal armies finally pried open the doorway into the Deep South.

In the years following the war, some veterans of the struggle began to return to Chattanooga to revisit the sites of the momentous events of 1863. Others took up paper and pen so that their version of events would be remembered. By the decade of the 1890s, veterans were returning in greater numbers as the battlefields were being preserved and monuments erected on those fields of strife. Many returned to share exploits with their families while others came alone to ponder the deeds done there. Some seemed to revel in the tales of the fighting while others seemed haunted by the memories of those comrades who never left.

But the strongest impulse was pursuing the idea of reconciliation. Though some on both sides still grumbled and harbored hostility toward their opponents, most veterans agreed to at least appear to let past animosities slip away, enduring what one former Confederate general cynically called "the blue gray gush." As a result, the various activities and dedications of parks and monuments passed without much controversy.

A noted exception occurred in 1895, but not between old enemies. John Turchin had long taken issue with Chickamauga and Chattanooga National Military Park's commission about the location of his brigade's assault on Missionary Ridge. The aging Turchin, a Russian émigré who donned the blue and who was always a controversial figure, was agitated by the placement of a monument to the 2nd Minnesota Infantry on the distinctive spur of Carroll's knoll, now known as the "DeLong Reservation of the new National Military Park." As if to add further insult, War Department plaques for Van Derveer's brigade—of which the 2nd Wisconsin had been a part—described its ascent, not Turchin's, at the site.

Turchin loudly proclaimed that the monument and descriptive tablets were misplaced—his brigade, alone, captured the position. Turchin's accusations clearly rankled one of the men most responsible for establishing the park and who now served as the park historian, Gen. Henry V. Boynton, who just happened to be the commander of the 35th Ohio Infantry, also of Van Derveer's brigade, and who was both severely wounded and later awarded the Medal of Honor for his role in that same charge.

John Turchin, a former officer in the Tsar's army, was an ardent free-thinker and abolitionist. He rose to brigadier general in the Union army. He was convinced that the markers and tablets for his brigade were misplaced. (ac)

Undaunted, Turchin was able to rally 37 veterans of his old command to his side to challenge the park. A war of words and ink followed. Equally unswayed, Boynton stated of Turchin's challenge, "I stake my reputation . . . on the assertion that no claim more nearly approaching utter nonsense has been made since work on this park began."

Turchin returned the contempt in full, claiming the park committee was "prejudiced," and sneering, "I never heard of Boynton during the war, but I see that he is pretty well advertised on the monuments on Missionary Ridge and Chickamauga Park nowadays." The following year, after a thorough review, the Secretary of War came down firmly on Boynton's side.

However, that ruling did not end the matter. Turchin renewed his push a few years later after Boynton resigned his park position to go back into active military service during the Spanish American War. Boynton's replacement was Ezra Carman, formerly of the Antietam National Battlefield in Maryland. Carman, who commanded the 13th New Jersey at Antietam, proved to be a tenacious, meticulous historian of Antietam, much as Boynton had been for Chickamauga-Chattanooga. Turchin clearly saw him as a fresh, unbiased observer.

At first, Carman, too, seemed to be entrenched, but he soon gave a sympathetic ear to Turchin's complaints. After the passing of General Turchin in 1901, Carman began more serious research into the controversy. In 1906, a year after Boynton's death, Carman actually began moving some of the DeLong reservation plaques farther north along Missionary Ridge. The push to move the 2nd Minnesota's monument off park land, however, proved to be a much more expensive proposition. It went nowhere.

With Carman's own death in 1909, the sequence of moves that Carman advocated across the park lost steam. From this point the controversies began to fade as their proponents passed away, leaving the War Department to finally state, "No further action be taken . . . and no changes of monuments, markers, or tablets, or of the location of monuments, markers or tablets be made. . . ."

Today the monuments, tablets and markers sit largely where Boynton placed them, silent witnesses to the struggle for Chattanooga.

Major Henry V. Boynton was wounded at the head of the 35th Ohio going up Missionary Ridge and was subsequently awarded the Medal of Honor for his actions there. As the military park's first historian, he was responsible for the placement of the monuments and markers, and as such, the target of Turchin's anger. (usahc)

A Corps is Formed

APPENDIX D

BY ERIC J. WITTENBERG

Near the end of August 1863, Gen. Robert E. Lee went to Richmond to consult with Confederate President Jefferson Davis, where they discussed the strategic picture after the twin defeats at Gettysburg and Vicksburg. On September 5, the Southern high command decided to detach two divisions of Lt. Gen. James Longstreet's First Corps and send them to reinforce Gen. Braxton Bragg's Army of Tennessee, with Longstreet in personal command of those troops. This meant that the effective strength of the Army of Northern Virginia would be reduced by approximately one-third, prompting one Confederate to note, "it has weakened this army smartly by sending Longstreet and his forces off." On September 9, the first contingents of Longstreet's corps left the Army of Northern Virginia, headed to Georgia to reinforce Bragg.

Just nine days later, on September 18, the great battle of Chickamauga began. Longstreet's men played a critical role in the Confederate victory there. General William Starke Rosecrans's badly beaten army retreated to Chattanooga. Bragg's army followed him there, cutting off Rosecrans's lines of supply and besieging the Union army.

After learning of the defeat of the Army of the Cumberland at Chickamauga, President Abraham Lincoln fretted. Lincoln had a lengthy discussion about the state of military affairs with Secretary of the Navy Gideon Welles that day. Welles wrote in his diary:

The decisive appearance of James Longstreet's men on the Chickamauga battlefield in mid-September—transferred from the Confederate Army of Northern Virginia—set in motion events that would lead to eventual formation of the Federal XX Corps, consisting of troops transferred from the Army of the Potomac. (cm)

I asked what Meade was doing with his immense army and Lee's skeleton and depleted show in front. He said he could not learn that Meade was doing anything, or wanted to do anything. "It is," said he, "the same old story of this Army of the Potomac. Imbecility, inefficiency—don't want to do—is defending the Capital. I inquired of Meade," said he, "what force was in front. Meade replied he thought there were 40,000 infantry. I replied he might have said 50,000, and if Lee with 50,000 could defend their capital against our 90,000,—and if defense is all our armies are to do,—we might, I thought, detach 50,000 from his command, and thus leave him with 40,000 to defend us. Oh," groaned the President, "it is terrible, terrible, this weakness, this indifference of our Potomac generals, with such armies of good and brave men." "Why," said I, "not rid yourself of Meade, who may be a good man and a good officer but is not a great general, has not breadth or strength, certainly is not the man for the position he occupies?" The escape of Lee with his army across the Potomac has distressed me almost beyond any occurrence of the War. And the impression made upon me in the personal interview shortly after was not what I wished, had inspired no confidence, though he is faithful and will obey orders; but he can't originate.

Meanwhile, things in Chattanooga were dire. The Army of the Cumberland faced the unhappy prospect of either starvation or surrender. Something had to be done, and quickly. Assistant Secretary of War Charles A. Dana, who was with the Army of the Cumberland in Chattanooga, sent a telegram to his superior, Edwin McMasters Stanton, late in the evening of September 23:

The net result of the campaign thus far is that we hold Chattanooga and the line of Tennessee River. It is true this result has been attended by a great battle with heavy losses, but it is certain that the enemy has suffered quite as severely as we have.

The first great object of the campaign, the possession of Chattanooga and the Tennessee line, still remains in our hands, and can be held by this army for from fifteen to twenty days against all efforts of the enemy, unless he should receive re-enforcements of overwhelming strength. But to render our hold here perfectly safe no time should be lost in pushing 20,000 to 25,000 efficient troops to Bridgeport. If such re-enforcements can be got there in season, everything is safe, and this place—indispensable alike to the defense of Tennessee and as the base of future operations in Georgia—will remain ours.

Alarmed, Stanton immediately called a conference of Lincoln, Secretary of State William H. Seward, Secretary of the Treasury Salmon P. Chase, and Union General in Chief Maj. Gen. Henry W. Halleck to discuss the situation.

Joe Hooker longed for redemption following his defeat at Chancellorsville, but his bickering with the War Department made him his own worst enemy. Only the influence of powerful political friends got him back on the battlefield. (loc)

After a lengthy discussion about how to reinforce the Army of the Cumberland, Stanton said, "I propose then to send 30,000 from the Army of the Potomac. There is no reason to expect that General Meade will attack Lee, although greatly superior in force; and his great numbers where they are, are useless. In five days, 30,000 could be put with Rosecrans." Chase noted in his diary that Lincoln and Halleck did not support the idea while Chase and Seward strongly advocated for the transfer. Halleck disagreed, claiming that it would take forty days to move a large force of men, artillery, and equipment to Chattanooga, and Lincoln agreed. Brigadier General Daniel C. McCallum, the director of the United States Military Railroad, agreed with Stanton and said that it could be done in a week.

Ultimately, the group decided that Halleck would telegraph Meade in the morning to ask if an immediate advance was planned. If not, then the XI and XII corps would be sent West at once, with Maj. Gen. Joseph Hooker, the former commander of the Army of the Potomac, in command, and with Maj. Gen. Daniel Butterfield as his chief of staff—a choice that delighted Chase and his fellow Radical Republicans. The die was cast.

The XI and XII corps made logical choices. Both had been battered at both Chancellorsville and Gettysburg, and the XI Corps had gained the unhappy nickname the "Flying Dutchmen"—the corps had the reputation of consisting largely of German immigrants who broke and ran at both battles. Consequently, after the battle of Gettysburg, Meade decided to break up the XI Corps, which he considered unreliable. On August 7, after the Army of the Potomac returned to Virginia from Pennsylvania, Brig. Gen. Alexander Schimmelfennig's 1st Division was permanently detached from the Army of the Potomac and was sent to serve at Charleston harbor, South Carolina. This left only about 6,000 officers and men in the two remaining divisions of the XI Corps—too small a force to stand as a separate corps.

Coincidentally, Halleck had summoned Meade to Washington on September 23. Meade immediately had boarded a train and had arrived 11:00 that evening, shortly before the meeting to discuss Dana's telegram. When he arrived, Meade had found Halleck still at his desk, fretting about the debacle at Chickamauga. Halleck then told Meade that Lincoln considered the Army of the Potomac to be too large to be a purely defensive one and had proposed to take part of it away. Meade had objected to this idea then left (before the president's meeting) to return to his army. Still believing that Lincoln was satisfied, Meade had continued making plans for a general advance by the army.

On September 24, Halleck wrote to Meade, "Please answer if you have positively determined to make any immediate movement. If not, prepare the Eleventh and Twelfth Corps to be sent to Washington as soon as cars can be sent to you." Meade complied, and the two corps prepared for their upcoming journey. More than 16,000 men left the Army of the Potomac and traveled nearly 1,200 miles to reinforce the Army of the Cumberland at Chattanooga.

Hooker was a controversial choice. An ardent abolitionist, Hooker was a favorite of the Radical Republican faction in Congress that was trying to dictate war policy to Lincoln. The Radical Republicans had objected to Hooker's removal from army command, and they wanted him returned to an important position, as he had languished without an assignment since the end of June. Hooker blamed the XI Corps for his defeat at Chancellorsville: after being flanked by Lt. Gen. Thomas J. "Stonewall" Jackson's Corps because of poor preparation and poor dispositions by Maj. Gen. O. O. Howard, the commander of the XI Corps, many of the corps's men broke and ran, although some elements of the corps fought long and hard that day.

Major General Henry W. Slocum, the commander of the XII Corps, in turn blamed Hooker for the debacle at Chancellorsville—as did Howard—and they were disgusted by his conduct there. A few days after Chancellorsville, Slocum, Maj. Gen. Darius N. Couch, commander of the II Corps, and Maj. Gen. John Sedgwick, commander of the VI Corps, sent word to Meade that they would gladly serve under him if Hooker were removed from command of the Army of the Potomac—and all three were senior to Meade. However, Lincoln offered command of the Army of the Potomac to Maj. Gen. John F. Reynolds, the highly esteemed leader of the I Corps, in mid-June, but Reynolds turned down the offer because Lincoln would not give him unfettered command of the army. For the time being, Hooker remained in place.

Hooker finally asked to be relieved of command on June 28 after Halleck denied Hooker's request to be given control over the Union garrison at Harpers Ferry, which was part of the Middle Military District, based in Baltimore, Maryland, and was not part of the Army of the Potomac or subject to Hooker's command. To his great surprise, Stanton approved the request to be relieved, and Meade was ordered to assume command of the army. Almost immediately, the Radical Republicans began agitating for Hooker's reinstatement to command. He was a reliable Republican abolitionist, he had the reputation of

Oliver Otis Howard would prove capable and, more importantly to his superiors in the West, non-political and non-troublesome—traits that would make him a far more palatable candidate for eventual promotion than the volatile Hooker. (loc)

being a fighter, and he was one of their favorites. By contrast, Meade was not a Republican and was considered to be too cautious and too politically unreliable to command an army.

Once the decision was made to send the XI and XII Corps to reinforce Rosecrans, Halleck summoned Howard to come to Washington. As one of Howard's biographers put it, "What thoughts [Howard] had on the subject he never indicated, and we may presume it is just as well. After Chancellorsville neither man cared much for the other . . . both perhaps had some justification for the dignified if undeniable enmity. For neither was it his finest hour." Upon his arrival, Howard reported to Hooker at his base of operations at the Willard Hotel. Hooker told Howard that his corps and Slocum's were to go west to reinforce Rosecrans as quickly as possible. After leaving Hooker, Howard called upon Lincoln.

Slocum, meanwhile—disgusted by the prospect of serving under Hooker's command again—offered his resignation rather than serve under "Fighting Joe." He penned a letter to Lincoln on September 25:

I have just been informed that I have been placed under command of Major General Joseph Hooker. My opinion of General Hooker both as an office and a gentleman is too well known to make it necessary for me to refer to it in this communication. The public service cannot be promoted by placing under his command an officer who has so little confidence in his ability as I have. Our relations are such that it would be degrading in me to accept any position under him. I have therefore to respectfully tender the resignation of my commission.

Lincoln refused to accept Slocum's resignation and placated him by promising a complete separation from Hooker as soon as possible. He wired Rosecrans with instructions to make it happen. The promise was made good. Slocum was assigned to guard the Nashville and Chattanooga Railroad with one division of the XII Corps, while the other division served under Hooker. Then, during the summer of 1864, Maj. Gen. William T. Sherman—by then the commander of the combined armies of the Western Theatre—appointed Slocum commander of the District of Vicksburg and commander of the XVII Corps, a duty he performed so well that Lt. Gen. Ulysses S. Grant resisted Slocum's transfer back to the Army of the Cumberland after Hooker's resignation.

As has been set forth fully in this book and its companion volume, *The Battle Above the Clouds*, both the XI and XII Corps performed well at Chattanooga, in particular, at Wauhatchie and again at Lookout Mountain. The combined force remained with the Army of the Cumberland after the great victory at Chattanooga.

On April 4, 1864, as he was preparing to launch his grand campaign to capture Atlanta, Sherman authorized the consolidation of the remnants of the XI and XII Corps to form the XX Corps. A newly organized division commanded by Gen. Daniel Adams Butterfield was assigned to join the XII Corps, which consisted of the veteran divisions of Brig. Gen. Alpheus S. Williams and Brig. Gen. John Geary. The two remaining divisions of the XI Corps were broken up and redistributed to the divisions of Williams, Geary, and Butterfield. The new organization retained the badge of the XII Corps. Each division consisted of three brigades, containing 52 regiments of infantry, 6 batteries of artillery, and numbering 21,280 officers and men. Sherman retained Hooker in command of the XX Corps and assigned it to the Army of the Cumberland.

The competent but fussy Henry Slocum would find a rhythm that suited him under William T. Sherman's command. (loc)

The XX Corps fought well throughout the Atlanta campaign, and its troops were the first to enter the city of Atlanta when it fell. However, when the commander of the Army of the Tennessee, Maj. Gen. James B. McPherson, was killed during the battle of Atlanta on July 22, 1864, Sherman appointed Howard to command the Army of the Tennessee over Hooker, who, as the senior corps commander, should have been next in line.

Hooker took offense to Sherman's choosing

a junior officer over him, and he still blamed Howard for his defeat at Chancellorsville, so he refused to serve under Howard's command. Miffed, Hooker wrote to Maj. Gen. George H. Thomas, the commander of the Army of the Cumberland, "I have just learned that Major General Howard my junior, has been assigned to the command of the Army of the Tennessee. If this is the case I request that I may be relieved from duty with this army. Justice and self-respect alike require my removal from an army in which rank and service are ignored."

Sherman told Halleck, "All are well pleased with General Howard's appointment but . . . General Hooker is offended because he thinks he is entitled to the command. I must be honest and say that he is not qualified or suited to it. He talks of quitting. . . . I shall not object. He is not indispensable to our success. He is welcome to my place if the President awards it, but I cannot name him to so important a command as the Army of the Tennessee."

When Lt. Gen. Ulysses S. Grant concurred with Sherman's assessment, Hooker's resignation was accepted, and he left the army.

Brigadier General Alpheus S. Williams, a former commander of the XII Corps, commanded the XX Corps for a month, from Hooker's resignation on July 28, 1864, until Slocum assumed command of the corps on August 27. To the joy of the soldiers of the old XII Corps, Slocum was elevated to army command before the "March to the Sea," and Williams again assumed command of the XX Corps, leading it on that march and through the Carolinas campaign. The final commander of the XX Corps was Maj. Gen. Joseph Mower, who led the corps from April 2, 1865, through the Grand Review in Washington, DC, in May, and until its disbandment on June 4, while Williams, whom Mower outranked, returned to divisional command within the XX Corps.

The XX Corps became an integral part of Sherman's victorious army, and Sherman relied on his "paper collar Easterners" by giving them

difficult assignments. The transplants from the Army of the Potomac—and the men of the XI Corps, in particular—vindicated their bad reputation through their fine service in the Western Theatre.

William T. Sherman (center, seated), surrounded by his eventual command team in the West: Oliver Otis Howard, John A. Logan, William B. Hazen, Jefferson C. Davis, Henry Warner Slocum, Joseph A. Mower. (loc)

Order of Battle
November 12-27, 1863.
THE CHATTANOOGA CAMPAIGN
Units and commands on detached duty are not listed.

OVERALL UNION FORCES
Maj. Gen. Ulysses S. Grant

ARMY OF THE CUMBERLAND
Maj. Gen. George H. Thomas

General Headquarters: *1st Ohio Sharpshooters • 10th Ohio Infantry*

FOURTH CORPS: Maj. Gen. Gordon Granger
FIRST DIVISION: Brig. Gen. Charles Cruft
Escort: *Co. E, 92nd Illinois Mounted Infantry*

Second Brigade: Brig. Gen. Walter C. Whitaker
96th Illinois • 35th Indiana • 8th Kentucky • 40th Ohio • 51st Ohio • 99th Ohio

Third Brigade: Col. William Grose
59th Illinois • 75th Illinois • 84th Illinois • 9th Indiana • 36th Indiana • 24th Ohio

SECOND DIVISION: Maj. Gen. Philip Sheridan
First Brigade: Col. Francis T. Sherman
*36th Illinois • 44th Illinois • 73rd Illinois • 74th Illinois • 88th Illinois
22nd Indiana • 2nd Missouri • 15th Missouri • 24th Wisconsin*

Second Brigade: Brig. Gen. George D. Wagner
*100th Illinois • 15th Indiana • 40th Indiana • 51st Indiana • 57th Indiana
58th Indiana • 26th Ohio • 97th Ohio*

Third Brigade: Col. Charles G. Harker
*22nd Illinois • 27th Illinois • 42nd Illinois • 51st Illinois • 79th Illinois
3rd Kentucky • 64th Ohio • 65th Ohio • 125th Ohio*

Artillery: Capt. Warren P. Edgarton
*M, 1st Illinois Lt. • 10th Indiana Battery • G, 1st Missouri Lt.
I, 1st Ohio Lt. • G, 4th US • M, 4th US*

THIRD DIVISION: Brig. Gen. Thomas J. Wood
First Brigade: Brig. Gen. August Willich
25th Illinois • 35th Illinois • 89th Illinois • 32nd Indiana • 68th Indiana
8th Kansas • 15th Ohio • 49th Ohio • 15th Wisconsin

Second Brigade: Brig. Gen. William B. Hazen
6th Indiana • 5th Kentucky • 6th Kentucky • 23rd Kentucky • 1st Ohio • 6th Ohio
41st Ohio • 93rd Ohio • 124th Ohio

Third Brigade: Brig. Gen. Samuel Beatty
79th Indiana • 86th Indiana • 9th Kentucky • 17th Kentucky • 13th Ohio
19th Ohio • 59th Ohio

Artillery: Capt. Cullen Bradley
Bridges's Battery, Illinois Lt. • 6th Ohio Battery • 20th Ohio Battery
Co. B, Pennsylvania Lt.

ELEVENTH CORPS: Maj. Gen. Oliver O. Howard
Independent Company: *8th New York Infantry*
SECOND DIVISION: Brig. Gen. Adolph von Steinwehr
First Brigade: Col. Adolphus Buschbeck
33rd New Jersey • 134th New York • 154th New York • 27th Pennsylvania
73rd Pennsylvania

Second Brigade: Col. Orland Smith
33rd Massachusetts • 136th New York • 55th Ohio • 73rd Ohio

THIRD DIVISION: Maj. Gen. Carl Schurz
First Brigade: Brig. Gen. Hector Tyndale
101st Illinois • 45th New York • 143rd New York • 61st Ohio • 82nd Ohio

Second Brigade: Col. Wladimir Krzyzanowski
58th New York • 119th New York • 141st New York • 26th Wisconsin

Third Brigade: Col. Frederick Hecker
80th Illinois • 82nd Illinois • 68th New York • 75th Pennsylvania

Artillery: Maj. Thomas W. Osborn
I, 1st New York Lt. • 13th New York Lt. • I, 1st Ohio Lt. • K, 1st Ohio Lt. • G, 4th US

TWELFTH CORPS: (only one division present)
SECOND DIVISION: Brig. Gen. John W. Geary

First Brigade: Col. Charles Candy
5th Ohio • 7th Ohio • 29th Ohio • 66th Ohio • 28th Pennsylvania • 147th Pennsylvania

Second Brigade: Col. George A. Cobham, Jr.
29th Pennsylvania • 109th Pennsylvania • 111th Pennsylvania

Third Brigade: Col. David Ireland
60th New York • 78th New York • 102nd New York • 137th New York • 149th New York

Artillery: Maj. John A. Reynolds
E, Pennsylvania Lt. • K, 5th US

FOURTEENTH CORPS: Maj. Gen. John M. Palmer
Escort: *Co. L, 1st Ohio Cavalry*
FIRST DIVISION: Brig. Gen. Richard W. Johnson
First Brigade: Brig. Gen. William P. Carlin
*104th Illinois • 38th Indiana • 42nd Indiana • 88th Indiana • 2nd Ohio
33rd Ohio • 94th Ohio • 10th Wisconsin*

Second Brigade: Col. Marshall F. Moore
*19th Illinois • 11th Michigan • 69th Ohio • 1/15th US • 2/15th US
1/16th US • 1/18th US • 2/18th US • 1/19th US*

Third Brigade: Brig. Gen. John C. Starkweather
*24th Illinois • 37th Indiana • 21st Ohio • 74th Ohio • 78th Pennsylvania
79th Pennsylvania • 1st Wisconsin • 21st Wisconsin*

Artillery:
C, 1st Illinois Lt. • A, 1st Michigan Lt. • H, 5th US[1]

SECOND DIVISION: Brig. Gen. Jefferson C. Davis
First Brigade: Brig. Gen. James D. Morgan
10th Illinois • 16th Illinois • 60th Illinois • 21st Kentucky • 10th Michigan

Second Brigade: Brig. Gen. John Beatty
34th Illinois • 78th Illinois • 98th Ohio • 108th Ohio • 113th Ohio • 121st Ohio

Third Brigade: Col. Daniel McCook
85th Illinois • 86th Illinois • 110th Illinois • 125th Illinois • 52nd Ohio

Artillery: Capt. William A. Hotchkiss
I, 2nd Illinois Lt. • 2nd Minnesota Lt. • 5th Wisconsin Lt.

THIRD DIVISION: Brig. Gen. Absalom Baird
First Brigade: Brig. Gen. John B. Turchin
*82nd Indiana • 11th Ohio • 17th Ohio • 31st Ohio • 36th Ohio • 89th Ohio
92nd Ohio*

Second Brigade: Col. Ferdinand Van Derveer
*75th Indiana • 87th Indiana • 101st Indiana • 2nd Minnesota • 9th Ohio
35th Ohio • 105th Ohio*

Third Brigade: Col. Edward Phelps
*10th Indiana • 74th Indiana • 4th Kentucky • 10th Kentucky • 18th Kentucky
14th Ohio • 38th Ohio*

Artillery: Capt. George R. Swallow
7th Indiana Lt. • 19th Indiana Lt. • I, 4th US

ENGINEER TROOPS: Brig. Gen. William F. Smith
Engineers:
*1st Michigan Engineers (detachment) • 13th Michigan • 21st Michigan
22nd Michigan • 18th Ohio*

ARTILLERY RESERVE: Brig. Gen. John M. Brannan
FIRST DIVISION: Col. James Barnett
First Brigade: Maj. Charles S. Cotter
B, 1st Ohio Lt. • C, 1st Ohio Lt. • E, 1st Ohio Lt. • F, 1st Ohio Lt.

Second Brigade: (no commander listed)
G, 1st Ohio Lt. • M, 1st Ohio Lt. • 19th Ohio Battery • 20th Ohio Battery

SECOND DIVISION: (no commander listed)
First Brigade: Capt. Josiah W. Church
*D, 1st Michigan Lt. • A, 1st Tennessee Lt. • 3rd Wisconsin Lt. • 8th Wisconsin Lt.
10th Wisconsin Lt.*

Second Brigade: Capt. Arnold Sutermeister
*4th Indiana Lt. • 8th Indiana Lt. • 11th Indiana Lt. • 21st Indiana Lt.
C, 1st Wisconsin Heavy Artillery*

CAVALRY CORPS: (mostly not present)
Second Brigade, Second Division: Col. Eli Long
98th Illinois Mounted Infantry • 17th Indiana Mounted Infantry • 2nd Kentucky Cavalry
4th Michigan Cavalry • 1st Ohio Cavalry • 3rd Ohio Cavalry • 4th Ohio Cavalry
10th Ohio Cavalry

Post of Chattanooga: Col. John G. Parkhurst
44th Indiana • 15th Kentucky • 9th Michigan

ARMY OF THE TENNESSEE
Maj. Gen. William T. Sherman

FIFTEENTH CORPS: Maj. Gen. Frank P. Blair
FIRST DIVISION: Brig. Gen. Peter J. Osterhaus
First Brigade: Brig. Gen. Charles R. Woods
13th Illinois • 3rd Missouri • 12th Missouri • 17th Missouri • 27th Missouri
29th Missouri • 31st Missouri • 32nd Missouri • 76th Ohio

Second Brigade: Col. James A. Williamson
4th Iowa • 9th Iowa • 25th Iowa • 26th Iowa • 30th Iowa • 31st Iowa

Artillery: Capt. Henry A. Griffiths
1st Iowa Lt. • F, 2nd Missouri Lt. • 4th Ohio Lt.

SECOND DIVISION: Brig. Gen. Morgan L. Smith
First Brigade: Brig. Gen. Giles A. Smith
55th Illinois • 116th Illinois • 127th Illinois • 6th Missouri • 8th Missouri
57th Ohio • 1/13th US

Second Brigade: Brig. Gen. Joseph A. Lightburn
83rd Indiana • 30th Ohio • 37th Ohio • 47th Ohio • 54th Ohio • 4th West Virginia

Artillery: (no commander listed)
A, 1st Illinois Lt. • B, 1st Illinois Lt. • H, 1st Illinois Lt.

FOURTH DIVISION: Brig. Gen. Hugh Ewing
First Brigade: Col. John M. Loomis
26th Illinois • 90th Illinois • 12th Indiana • 100th Indiana

Second Brigade: Brig. Gen. John M. Corse
40th Illinois • 103rd Illinois • 6th Iowa • 46th Ohio

Third Brigade: Col. Joseph R. Cockerill
48th Illinois • 97th Indiana • 99th Indiana • 53rd Ohio • 70th Ohio

Artillery: Capt. Henry Richardson
F, 1st Illinois Lt. • I, 1st Illinois Lt. • D, 1st Missouri Lt.

SEVENTEENTH CORPS: (no commander listed)
SECOND DIVISION: Brig. Gen. John E. Smith
First Brigade: Col. Jesse I. Alexander
63rd Illinois • 48th Indiana • 59th Indiana • 4th Minnesota • 18th Wisconsin

Second Brigade: Col. Green B. Raum
56th Illinois • 17th Iowa • 10th Missouri • 24th Missouri • 80th Ohio

Third Brigade: Brig. Gen. Charles L. Matthies
93rd Illinois • 5th Iowa • 10th Iowa • 26th Missouri

Artillery: Capt. Henry Dillon
Cogswell's Illinois Battery • 6th Wisconsin Lt. • 12th Wisconsin Lt.

* * *

CONFEDERATE ARMY OF TENNESSEE[2]
Gen. Braxton Bragg

General Headquarters: *1st Louisiana Infantry (regulars) • 1st Louisiana Cavalry*

LONGSTREET'S CORPS: Lt. Gen. James Longstreet[3]
McLAWS'S DIVISION: Maj. Gen. Lafayette McLaws
Kershaw's Brigade: Brig. Gen. Joseph B. Kershaw
*2nd South Carolina • 3rd South Carolina • 7th South Carolina • 8th South Carolina
15th South Carolina • 3rd South Carolina Battalion*

Humphreys's Brigade: Brig. Gen. Benjamin C. Humphreys
13th Mississippi • 17th Mississippi • 18th Mississippi • 21st Mississippi

Wofford's Brigade: Col. S. Z. Ruff
*16th Georgia • 18th Georgia • 24th Georgia • Cobb's Legion
3rd Georgia Battalion Sharpshooters*

Bryan's Brigade: Brig. Gen. Goode Bryan
10th Georgia • 50th Georgia • 51st Georgia • 53rd Georgia

Artillery: Maj. Austin Leyton
Peeples's Georgia Battery • Wolihin's Georgia Battery • York's Georgia Battery

HOOD'S DIVISION: Brig. Gen. Micah Jenkins
Jenkins's Brigade: Col. John Bratton
1st South Carolina • 2nd South Carolina Rifles • 5th South Carolina
6th South Carolina • Hampton Legion • Palmetto Sharpshooters

Law's Brigade: Brig. Gen. Evander M. Law
4th Alabama • 15th Alabama • 44th Alabama • 47th Alabama • 48th Alabama

Robertson's Brigade: Brig. Gen. Jerome B. Robertson
3rd Arkansas • 1st Texas • 4th Texas • 5th Texas

Anderson's Brigade: Brig. Gen. George T. Anderson
7th Georgia • 8th Georgia • 9th Georgia • 11th Georgia • 59th Georgia

Benning's Brigade: Brig. Gen. Henry L. Benning
2nd Georgia • 15th Georgia • 17th Georgia • 20th Georgia

Artillery: Col. E. Porter Alexander
Fickling's South Carolina Battery • Jordan's Virginia Battery • Moody's Louisiana Battery
Parker's Virginia Battery • Taylor's Virginia Battery • Woolfolk's Virginia Battery

HARDEE'S CORPS: Lt. Gen. William J. Hardee
CHEATHAM'S DIVISION: Maj. Gen. William H. T. Walker
Jackson's Brigade: Brig. Gen. John K. Jackson
1st Georgia • 5th Georgia • 47th Georgia • 65th Georgia
2nd Battalion Georgia Sharpshooters • 5th Mississippi • 8th Mississippi

Moore's Brigade: Brig. Gen. John C. Moore
37th Alabama • 40th Alabama • 42nd Alabama

Walthall's Brigade: Brig. Gen. Edward C. Walthall
24th Mississippi • 27th Mississippi • 29th Mississippi • 30th Mississippi
34th Mississippi

Wright's Brigade: Brig. Gen. Marcus J. Wright
*8th Tennessee • 16th Tennessee • 28th Tennessee • 38th Tennessee
51st/52nd Tennessee • Murray's Tennessee Battalion*

Artillery: Maj. Melancton Smith
*Fowler's Alabama Battery • McCants's Florida Battery • Scogin's Georgia Battery
Turner's (Smith's) Mississippi Battery*

HINDMAN'S DIVISION: Brig. Gen. J. Patton Anderson
Anderson's Brigade: Col. William F. Tucker
*7th Mississippi • 9th Mississippi • 10th Mississippi • 41st Mississippi
44th Mississippi • 9th Mississippi Battalion Sharpshooters*

Manigault's Brigade: Brig. Gen. Arthur M. Manigault
24th Alabama • 28th Alabama • 34th Alabama • 10th/19th South Carolina

Deas's Brigade: Brig. Gen. Zachariah C. Deas
*19th Alabama • 22nd Alabama • 25th Alabama • 33rd Alabama • 50th Alabama
17th Alabama Battalion Sharpshooters*

Vaughan's Brigade: Brig. Gen. Alfred J. Vaughan, Jr.
11th Tennessee • 12th/47th Tennessee • 13th/154th Tennessee • 29th Tennessee

Artillery: Maj. Alfred R. Courtney
*Dent's Alabama Battery • Garrity's Alabama Battery • Doscher's (Scott's) Tennessee Battery
Hamilton's (Water's) Alabama Battery*

BUCKNER'S DIVISION: Brig. Gen. Bushrod R. Johnston[4]
Johnson's Brigade: Col. John S. Fulton
17th/23rd Tennessee • 25th/44th Tennessee • 63rd Tennessee

Gracie's Brigade: Brig. Gen. Archibald Gracie, Jr.
*41st Alabama • 43rd Alabama • 1st, 2nd, 3rd, & 4th Battalions, Hilliard's
(Alabama) Legion*

Reynolds's Brigade: Brig. Gen. A. W. Reynolds[5]
58th North Carolina • 60th North Carolina • 54th Virginia • 63rd Virginia

Artillery: Maj. Samuel C. Williams
*Bullen's (Darden's) Mississippi Battery • Jeffries's Virginia Battery
Kolb's Alabama Battery*

WALKER'S DIVISION: Brig. Gen. States Rights Gist
Maney's Brigade: Brig. Gen. George Maney
1st/27th Tennessee • 4th Tennessee • 6th/9th Tennessee • 41st Tennessee
56th Tennessee • 24th Tennessee Battalion Sharpshooters

Gist's Brigade: Col. James McCullough
46th Georgia • 8th Georgia Battalion • 16th South Carolina • 24th South Carolina

Wilson's Brigade: Col. Claudius C. Wilson
25th Georgia • 29th Georgia • 30th Georgia • 26th Georgia Battalion
1st Georgia Battalion Sharpshooters

Artillery: Maj. Robert Martin
Bledsoe's Missouri Battery • Ferguson's South Carolina Battery • Howell's Georgia Battery

BRECKINRIDGE'S CORPS: Maj. Gen. John C. Breckinridge
CLEBURNE'S DIVISION: Maj. Gen. Patrick R. Cleburne
Liddell's Brigade: Col. Daniel C. Govan
2nd/15th Arkansas • 5th/13th Arkansas • 6th/7th Arkansas • 19th/24th Arkansas

Smith's Brigade: Col. Hiram B. Granbury
6th/10th Texas Infantry/15th Texas Dismounted Cavalry • 7th Texas Infantry
17th/18th/24th/25th Texas Dismounted Cavalry

Polk's Brigade: Brig. Gen. Lucius Polk
1st Arkansas • 3rd/5th Confederate • 2nd Tennessee • 35th/48th Tennessee

Lowrey's Brigade: Brig. Gen. Mark P. Lowrey
16th Alabama • 33rd Alabama • 45th Alabama • 32nd/45th Mississippi
15th Mississippi Battalion Sharpshooters

Artillery: (no commander listed)
Key's Arkansas Battery • Douglas's Texas Battery
Goldthwaite's (Semple's) Alabama Battery • Shannon's (Swett's) Mississippi Battery

STEWART'S DIVISION: Maj. Gen. Alexander P. Stewart
Adam's Brigade: Col. Randall L. Gibson
13th/20th Louisiana • 16th/25th Louisiana • 19th Louisiana
4th Louisiana Battalion • 14th Louisiana Battalion Sharpshooters

Strahl's Brigade: Brig. Gen. Otho F. Strahl
4th/5th Tennessee • 18th Tennessee • 24th Tennessee • 31st Tennessee • 33rd Tennessee

Clayton's Brigade: Col. J. T. Holtzclaw
18th Alabama • 32nd Alabama • 36th Alabama • 38th Alabama • 58th Alabama

Stovall's Brigade: Brig. Gen. Marcellus A. Stovall
40th Georgia • 41st Georgia • 42nd Georgia • 43rd Georgia • 52nd Georgia

Artillery: Capt. Henry C. Semple
Anderson's (Dawson's) Georgia Battery • Rivers's (Humphreys's) Arkansas Battery
Oliver's Alabama Battery • Stanford's Mississippi Battery

BRECKINRIDGE'S DIVISION: Maj. Gen. William B. Bate
Lewis's Brigade: Brig. Gen. Joseph H. Lewis
2nd Kentucky • 4th Kentucky • 5th Kentucky • 6th Kentucky • 8th Kentucky
Morgan's detachment dismounted cavalry

Bate's Brigade: Col. R. C. Tyler
37th Georgia • 4th Georgia Battalion Sharpshooters • 10th Tennessee
15th/37th Tennessee • 20th Tennessee • 30th Tennessee • 1st Tennessee Battalion

Florida Brigade: Col. Jesse J. Finley
1st/3rd Florida • 4th Florida • 6th Florida • 7th Florida • 1st Florida Dismounted Cavalry

Artillery: Capt. C. H. Slocomb
Gracey's (Cobb's) Kentucky Battery • Mebane's Tennessee Battery
Vaught's (Slocomb's) Louisiana Battery

STEVENSON'S DIVISION: Maj. Gen. Carter L. Stevenson
Brown's Brigade: Brig. Gen. John C. Brown
3rd Tennessee • 18th/20th Tennessee • 32nd Tennessee • 45th Tennessee
23rd Tennessee Battalion

Cumming's Brigade: Brig. Gen. Alfred Cumming
34th Georgia • 36th Georgia • 39th Georgia • 56th Georgia

Pettus's Brigade: Brig. Gen. Edmund W. Pettus
20th Alabama • 23rd Alabama • 30th Alabama • 31st Alabama • 46th Alabama

Artillery: Capt. Robert Cobb
Baxter's Tennessee Battery • Carnes's Tennessee Battery
Van Den Corput's Georgia Battery • Rowan's Georgia Battery

CAVALRY[6]
KELLY'S DIVISION: Brig. Gen. John H. Kelly
First Brigade: Col. William B. Wade
1st Confederate • 3rd Confederate • 8th Confederate • 10th Confederate

Second Brigade: Col. J. Warren Grigsby
*2nd Kentucky • 3rd Kentucky • 9th Kentucky • Allison's Tennessee Squadron
Hamilton's Tennessee Battalion • Rucker's Legion*

Artillery: (no commander listed)
*Huggins's Tennessee Battery • Huwald's Tennessee Battery • White's Tennessee Battery
Wiggins's Arkansas Battery*

---

1 Temporarily attached to Sheridan's division of the Fourth Corps

2 Organization shown from November 12, 1863

3 From Virginia, detached to East Tennessee in early November

4 This division, except for Reynolds's brigade and the artillery, was sent to East Tennessee on November 22.

5 Attached to Stevenson's division after November 22

6 The bulk of Maj. Gen. Joseph Wheeler's Cavalry Corps was operating in East Tennessee, first with Stevenson and then with Longstreet. Only Kelly's division remained with Bragg; of that force, Kelly and Wade's brigade was operating around Cleveland, Tennessee.

A Confederate gunner
stands ready at the base of
the Maryland Monument on
Orchard Knob. Maryland,
who had only a handful
of troops present for the
battles of Chattanooga,
follows Kentucky's tradition
in honoring the men of both
sides who fought here. (loc)

Suggested Reading

THE CHATTANOOGA CAMPAIGN

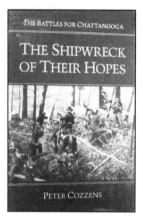

The Shipwreck of Their Hopes:
The Battles for Chattanooga
Peter Cozzens
University of Illinois, 1994
ISBN: 0-252-01922-9

Peter Cozzens's study of the campaign is very tactical, with a tight focus on regimental movements and actions. It is the third book of three focusing on the campaigns of the Army of the Cumberland. His focus here remains primarily on that army, though he does not skimp in detailing the actions of either the Confederates or of those Federals brought in to reinforce the Army of the Cumberland.

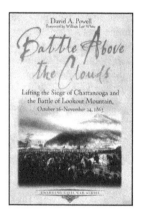

Battle Above the Clouds: Lifting the Siege of Chattanooga and the Battle of Lookout Mountain, October 26 – November 24, 1863
David A. Powell
Savas Beatie, 2017 (Emerging Civil War Series)
ISBN: 978-1-61121-377-5

The companion volume to *All Hell Can't Stop Them*, *Battle Above the Clouds* recounts the interlude between the Battle of Chickamauga and the beginning of U. S. Grant's orchestrated campaign to end the siege of Chattanooga. As such, it covers not only the opening of the Cracker Line, culminating in the rare night battle of Wauhatchie, but also provides the only single-volume coverage of that most spectacular of Civil War battles, Lookout Mountain.

A Chickamauga Memorial: The Establishment of
America's First Civil War National Military Park
Timothy B. Smith
University of Tennessee Press, 2009
ISBN: 1-57233-579-X

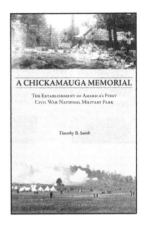

Timothy Smith, one of the foremost experts on
the history of Civil War battlfields, documents the
conception, creation, and early story of the nation's
first National Military Park at Chickamauga and
Chattanooga.

Mountains Touched with Fire:
Chattanooga Besieged, 1863
Wiley Sword
St. Martin's Press, 1995
ISBN: 0-312-11859-7

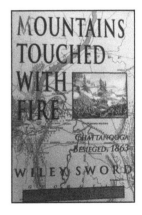

Wiley Sword's study of the same conflict, appearing
the year after Cozzens's work, is focused a bit more
on the upper echelons of command for both sides;
it is more of an operational study than a tactical
one. Both volumes offer valuable insights into
the events known collectively as the Chattanooga
campaign, but perhaps Sword's language is slightly
more lyrical and evocative.

Bushwhacking on a Grand Scale:
The Battle of Chickamauga, September 18-20, 1863
William Lee White
Savas Beatie, 2013 (Emerging Civil War Series)
ISBN: 978-1-61121-158-0

The battle for Missionary Ridge was but one part of a larger story, the months-long struggle for control of Chattanooga. The Chickamauga Campaign was the first part of that story. *Bushwhacking on a Grand Scale* serves as a worthy introduction to that campaign, which culminated in the second-largest battle of the Civil War; and helps to explain some of the earlier strategic decisions surrounding the fighting for Chattanooga.

Six Armies in Tennessee:
The Chickamauga and Chattanooga Campaigns
Steven E. Woodworth
University of Nebraska, 1998
ISBN: 0-8032-4778-8

Steven Woodworth's narrative is a high-level strategic and operational view of the entire struggle, beginning with the Tullahoma Campaign in June 1863, and concluding with the Confederate defeat at Chattanooga at the end of November. In covering such a broad sweep in less than 250 pages, Woodworth's narrative remains focused on decision-making within the upper-echelons of command, but his insight into those decisions make this book essential for comprehending the strategic narrative.

The Chattanooga Campaign
Steven E. Woodworth and Charles D. Grear, eds.
Southern Illinois University Press, 2012
ISBN: 978-0-8093-3119-5

*Gateway to the Confederacy: New Perspectives on the
Chickamauga and Chattanooga Campaigns, 1862-1863*
Evan C. Jones and Wiley Sword, eds.
Louisiana State University, 2014
ISBN: 978-0-8071-5509-7

Each of these books are essay collections, not
narrative histories of the campaigns in question.
Each volume includes ten chapters penned by
different experts. The insights offered range
from the pondering of campaign considerations
to explorations of Civil War memory and
preservation; taken together they richly reward
the reader with some of the best short historical
writing on the subject of Chattanooga.

About the Author

David A. Powell is a graduate of the Virginia Military Institute (1983) with a BA in history. He has published numerous articles in various magazines, and more than fifteen historical simulations of different battles. For the past fifteen years, David's focus has been on the epic battle of Chickamauga, and he is nationally recognized for his tours of that important battlefield. His first published book was *The Maps of Chickamauga* (Savas Beatie, 2009). Next came *Failure in the Saddle: Nathan Bedford Forrest, Joe Wheeler, and the Confederate Cavalry in the Chickamauga Campaign* (Savas Beatie, 2011). Most recently, he has concluded a narrative history of the Chickamauga Campaign in three volumes: volume I, *The Chickamauga Campaign: A Mad Irregular Battle* (2014); volume II, *The Chickamauga Campaign: Glory or the Grave* (2015); and volume III, *The Chickamauga Campaign: Barren Victory* (2016). *Battle Above the Clouds: Lifting the Siege of Chattanooga and the Battle of Lookout Mountain*, the precursor to this volume, was published in 2017. David, his wife Anne, and their brace of bloodhounds live and work in the northwest suburbs of Chicago, Illinois. He is Vice President of Airsped, Inc., a specialized delivery firm.